THE BEDFORD SERIES IN HISTORY AND CULTURE

The Rise of Conservatism in America, 1945–2000

A Brief History with Documents

Related Titles in
THE BEDFORD SERIES IN HISTORY AND CULTURE
Advisory Editors: Lynn Hunt, *University of California, Los Angeles*
David W. Blight, *Yale University*
Bonnie G. Smith, *Rutgers University*
Natalie Zemon Davis, *Princeton University*
Ernest R. May, *Harvard University*

THE BEDFORD SERIES IN HISTORY AND CULTURE

The Rise of Conservatism in America, 1945–2000

A Brief History with Documents

Ronald Story

University of Massachusetts Amherst

Bruce Laurie

University of Massachusetts Amherst

BEDFORD/ST. MARTIN'S   Boston ♦ New York

To David Montgomery and Dan Taylor

For Bedford/St. Martin's

Publisher for History: Mary V. Dougherty
Director of Development for History: Jane Knetzger
Developmental Editor: Shannon Hunt
Editorial Assistant: Laurel Damashek
Production Supervisor: Jennifer Peterson
Production Associate: Maureen O'Neill
Executive Marketing Manager: Jenna Bookin Barry
Project Management: Books By Design, Inc.
Cover Design: Billy Boardman
Text Design: Claire Seng-Niemoeller
Indexer: Books By Design, Inc.
Cover Art: *Ronald Reagan at the Republican National Convention, Detroit, Michigan, 1980.* Corbis.
Composition: Stratford Publishing Services, Inc.
Printing and Binding: RR Donnelley & Sons Company

President: Joan E. Feinberg
Editorial Director: Denise B. Wydra
Director of Marketing: Karen Melton Soeltz
Director of Editing, Design, and Production: Marcia Cohen
Manager, Publishing Services: Emily Berleth

Library of Congress Control Number: 2006935059

Copyright © 2008 by Bedford/St. Martin's

Manufactured in the United States of America.

For information, write: Bedford/St. Martin's, 75 Arlington Street, Boston, MA 02116 (617-399-4000)

ISBN-10: 0-312-45064-8
ISBN-13: 978-0-312-45064-9

Acknowledgments

Acknowledgments and copyrights are continued at the back of the book on pages 179–180, which constitute an extension of the copyright page.

Foreword

The Bedford Series in History and Culture is designed so that readers can study the past as historians do.

The historian's first task is finding the evidence. Documents, letters, memoirs, interviews, pictures, movies, novels, or poems can provide facts and clues. Then the historian questions and compares the sources. There is more to do than in a courtroom, for hearsay evidence is welcome, and the historian is usually looking for answers beyond act and motive. Different views of an event may be as important as a single verdict. How a story is told may yield as much information as what it says.

Along the way the historian seeks help from other historians and perhaps from specialists in other disciplines. Finally, it is time to write, to decide on an interpretation and how to arrange the evidence for readers.

Each book in this series contains an important historical document or group of documents, each document a witness from the past and open to interpretation in different ways. The documents are combined with some element of historical narrative—an introduction or a biographical essay, for example—that provides students with an analysis of the primary source material and important background information about the world in which it was produced.

Each book in the series focuses on a specific topic within a specific historical period. Each provides a basis for lively thought and discussion about several aspects of the topic and the historian's role. Each is short enough (and inexpensive enough) to be a reasonable one-week assignment in a college course. Whether as classroom or personal reading, each book in the series provides firsthand experience of the challenge—and fun—of discovering, recreating, and interpreting the past.

Lynn Hunt
David W. Blight
Bonnie G. Smith
Natalie Zemon Davis
Ernest R. May

Preface

The Rise of Conservatism in America, 1945–2000 provides a brief documentary record of the most important political development in modern U.S. history: the emergence of a powerful new brand of conservatism, committed to a dramatic reorientation of all aspects of American government, culture, politics, diplomacy, and economics. Few students fully grasp the roots, scope, and complexity of the conservative movement even though it arose in earnest more than a half-century ago. Through imagination, tenacity, political skill, resources, and sheer force of will, the conservatives have amassed an impressive list of accomplishments. We hope this collection will contribute to a greater understanding of their achievement. At the very least it should stand as a record of how to get things done.

The introduction gives students the necessary background to understand why and how conservatism took hold in the United States, beginning with the backlash against New Deal liberalism and tracing the political, economic, and social circumstances that encouraged the spread of conservative thought. It contextualizes a document collection that spans fifty-three years, from an editorial on the Taft-Hartley Act, in our view the true opening shot in the conservative counter-revolution, to the 2000 election of George W. Bush, which demonstrated the sectional political realignment underlying the conservative ascendancy. To show the widespread support of the movement, we purposely include a variety of sources—speeches, books, essays, resolutions, platforms, campaign brochures, policy papers, cartoons. Together, they illustrate a range of issues (deregulation, subversion, crime, labor unions) and interests (the Soviet threat, gun rights, Equal Rights Amendment).

The documents capture key events in the conservative movement: the founding of *National Review* and of Moral Majority; the tax revolt; and the disintegration of the Solid Democratic South. They also give voice to the disparate groups like the John Birch Society, Southern Baptists, and military leaders that encompassed the movement. Speeches from some of conservatism's famous figures, such as Joseph McCarthy, Richard Nixon, Barry Goldwater, and Ronald Reagan, complement the statements of visionaries such as William F. Buckley and George Gilder. A headnote for each selection, a chronology of the movement, and questions for consideration make the documents accessible and useful tools for learning and teaching. Since the selections are necessarily brief to fit within the framework of a survey course, a selected bibliography encourages further exploration of the topic.

This volume is a collaboration. The two of us don't agree on everything and have argued about what to include and what to say, as will most readers given the sometimes controversial, sometimes emotional nature of this topic. But we began this undertaking with a genuine curiosity as to how this tremendous phenomenon came about. One outside reader complained, gratifyingly, that we seem too objective. We hope the same will be said of the finished product.

ACKNOWLEDGMENTS

The following reviewers of the first draft offered constructive criticism and helpful advice: Christine Erickson, Indiana University–Purdue University Fort Wayne; W. Taylor Fain, University of North Carolina Wilmington; Kevin Kruse, Princeton University; John Putman, San Diego State University; Robert Saxe, Rhodes College; Bruce Schulman, Boston University; and Victor Silverman, Pomona College. We wish to thank the following people at Bedford for their valuable contributions to this volume: Mary Dougherty, publisher for history; Jane Knetzger, director of development for history; Laurel Damashek, editorial assistant; and Emily Berleth, manager of publishing services. Series editor David Blight was an invaluable supporter and promoter of the project from the beginning. A special word of gratitude goes to Shannon Hunt, our wonderful editor, whose intelligence, attention, skill, and good humor helped make this a better, more serviceable book.

Ronald Story and Bruce Laurie

Contents

APPENDIXES

THE BEDFORD SERIES IN HISTORY AND CULTURE

The Rise of Conservatism in America, 1945–2000

A Brief History with Documents

PART ONE

Introduction: The Making of a Movement

The central story of American politics since World War II is the emergence of the conservative movement. After World War II American conservatism stood for limited government in domestic, economic, and social affairs and aggressive government in foreign affairs. Conservatives fought to restrict government activism at home with the goal of maximizing economic and personal freedom for both individuals and businesses. They favored the use of the free market instead of government to distribute economic resources and sustain economic growth. This traditional aspect of conservatism took on a new urgency after the introduction of the New Deal, the reforms carried out by the Democratic party in the 1930s that produced Social Security and the modern welfare state, as well as union-friendly labor laws and a long list of federal agencies that regulated business enterprise. The New Deal not only defined modern liberalism, but also provided postwar conservatism with its domestic mission: to dismantle liberalism's social programs and the progressive tax policies that paid for them. The advent of the cold war between the United States and the Soviet Union, moreover, led to the end of conservatism's traditional association with isolationism and suspicion of a strong military establishment. Fear of Soviet-style communism—atheistic, totalitarian, socialist, and heavily armed—turned conservatism into a force for an aggressive foreign policy aimed at collapsing communism on a worldwide scale.

The movement itself consisted of a range of ideological organizations and interest groups that influenced politicians and public policy. Groups such as the National Association of Manufacturers—the conservative business lobby—and the American Legion—the conservative veterans' group—had few members immediately after World War II and were not necessarily associated with either major party, although they tended to favor Republicans. In the early 1970s, however, the number of conservative organizations multiplied, branching out to include think tanks, media groups, and myriad single-issue lobbies. By the turn of the 1970s the movement expanded from economic conservatism and militant anticommunism to social conservatism. It embraced the personalities and groups associated with the more conservative religious denominations who were out to enforce what they called "traditional family values." The conservative movement was by that time synonymous with the Republican party; its operatives, some observers believe, displaced traditional party leaders. The movement helped produce the modern Republican majority in politics and the public policies of contemporary conservatism.

This unprecedented upsurge of conservatism has virtually erased the political terminology of the New Deal era. Today, one seldom hears of *consensus*, the term used to describe the middle-of-the-road politics of the 1950s, or of the New Deal coalition, the groups of white southerners, white ethnic workers, African Americans, and liberal intellectuals that underwrote the dominance of the Democratic party from the 1930s through the 1960s. The conservative movement, like the New Deal coalition, is an electoral alliance, but it differs in degree and kind. Its electoral base is more racially uniform but still diverse, uniting business leaders with southern suburbanites with northern industrial workers who were once reliably Democratic. It enjoys a much wider organizational reach than the New Deal coalition, stretching from gun clubs and evangelical churches to corporate political action committees. This impressive assemblage of voters, groups, and operatives affiliated with the Republican party has left a deep imprint on both public policy and public life.

No one, least of all the triumphant New Dealers of the late 1940s and 1950s, foresaw the conservative movement. Even when they lost the White House to the Republicans in 1952 and 1956, Democrats generally retained their grip on one or both houses of Congress and continued to set the tone of national politics. Conservative Republicans looked on in dismay as the Eisenhower administration not only failed to reverse the social legislation of the New Deal but virtually capitulated to Democratic liberalism. It accepted liberal domestic programs as a fact of political life and rejected the aggressive foreign policy of rolling back communist governments in favor of continuing the Truman administration's more moderate course of containing their advances. Nonetheless, conservatism grew quietly through the Eisenhower years and then surged into a major force.

Historians and political scientists dispute the date of that seismic change in the nation's political culture. Some point to the election of 1964, when Republican standard-bearer Barry Goldwater lost the presidential election but provided a rallying point for the men and women who would become leaders of the Right in the next decade. Others point to the rise of political organizers at the national level in the mid-1970s. Another school of thought looks to the grassroots, stressing Southern anti-integrationists, the rise of the John Birch Society in places like Southern California, or the popular backlash against the counterculture, urban riots, and antiwar movement of the late 1960s. Still another point of view emphasizes the emergence of the Christian Right in grassroots organizations during the 1990s. Each of these perspectives is valid.

This book demonstrates the rise of the movement in three distinct stages. Stage 1, "First Steps," documents the movement's origin by examining the work of conservative politicians and intellectuals when the conservative movement was in its formative stage: developing ideas and an agenda but only a patchy political base. Stage 2, "Expanding the Base," charts how conservatism took firmer organizational shape from the Goldwater campaign through the Nixon and Carter administrations. This section highlights the activities of a group of political activists drawn together in the Goldwater campaign. In the early 1970s they mimicked the Democrats by encouraging the formation of policy groups and think tanks to develop conservative social and economic programs and a more aggressive foreign policy.

Conservative operatives pioneered new forms of fund-raising and constructed national organizations focused on electoral politics. They also built alliances with single-issue groups that started from the grassroots, like the National Rifle Association, or emerged from leadership coalitions, like the Moral Majority. Such groups tended to reflect strong opposition to the liberal social policies of the Democratic party in the mid-1960s or widespread dismay over the social turmoil in the second half of the 1960s over civil rights and the war in Vietnam. It was in this middle stage that the Right substantially expanded its base, mobilizing voters in the West and upper Midwest, as well as in the South, a longtime target of conservative activists. It was in the South that the politics of race had periodically thrust white voters to the right and sometimes propelled them completely out of the Democratic party.

Republicans elected their modern hero, Ronald Reagan, to the presidency in this period, with only minimal help from the Christian Right, arguably the last conservative group to organize. We document the rise of the Christian Right in Stage 3—or what we call "Clean Sweep"—because it was in the 1990s that the conservative movement as we know it was completed despite ongoing factional tensions. This section provides material on conservative judges and radio talk-show hosts whose daily programs reach tens of millions of listeners. It also covers grassroots movements organized in defense of "traditional family values," the clarion of Christian groups grown militant over abortion, gay rights, and stem cell research. During the 1990s Protestants were joined by large numbers of Roman Catholics, who earlier had operated independently. This made the Christian Right more broadly Christian, more fully coordinated, and more powerful.

No single force accounts for this conservative ascendance. Movement operatives and fund-raisers supplied organizational know-how and money; think tanks and journals offered a rich variety of policies and programs. But conservative ideas and operatives did not in and of themselves produce a winning coalition. Population shifts to the Sunbelt region of the South and Southwest from northern Frostbelt states meant more voters for conservative Republicanism than liberal Democracy because of the long tradition of conservatism in the Deep South and a growing conservative constituency in the region's burgeoning suburbs. Although Democrats in both groups may well have warmed to Republican-style conservatism regardless of events, many people were tugged to the right in reaction to the civil rights, antiwar, and women's movements and by the riots and crime waves that rocked urban areas. Also, in the 1970s the prolonged economic slump in President Jimmy Carter's administration and the Democratic president's failed attempt to free American hostages taken by Islamic radicals in Iran[1] dampened the spirits of traditional Democratic supporters and alienated independent voters.

Conservative Republicans deftly exploited the Democratic party's vulnerability. They not only embraced such grassroots movements as the tax revolt, the anti–gun control movement, and the campaign against the Equal Rights Amendment, but promised to beef up the military, crack down on crime, and halt the court-ordered busing of schoolchildren to achieve racial balance in the schools. Their alliance with the Christian Right in the ensuing decade gave the Republicans an even broader coalition and a deeper base.

FIRST STEPS, 1945–1968

As World War II drew to a close in 1945, there was no conservative movement and not much conservative sentiment. The overwhelming majority of Americans embraced the New Deal and even showed some support for the Fair Deal, the program created by Roosevelt's successor, Harry S. Truman, that extended the party's platform to civil rights and national health insurance. However, signs of trouble with the New Deal coalition and with Truman's Fair Deal appeared as early as 1946. The wave of strikes that swept through basic industry inconvenienced a people yearning for quiet in the aftermath of the war and shook the Republicans from their torpor. The party of business and isolationism campaigned with the slogan "Had enough?" in reference to the labor unrest and presumed betrayal at Yalta, where FDR allegedly ceded Eastern Europe to Russian dictator Joseph Stalin's despotic communist government. Republicans took both houses of Congress and began to dismantle the New Deal's social legislation, their signal achievement being the Taft-Hartley Act of 1947. Repassed over President Truman's veto, this controversial measure, known in labor circles as the "slave labor law," relaxed protections for unionists enshrined in the Wagner Act of 1935 and sanctioned anti-union laws in the states, a big concession to the Democratic South. The advance of the New Deal envisioned in Truman's Fair Deal had been blunted (Document 1).

Perhaps even more troubling for the helmsmen of the Democratic party, not all unionists were unhappy about the weakening of their organizations. The journalist Samuel Lubell, in the early 1950s, reported unease in the ranks of labor. The union men he interviewed betrayed a quiet anxiety, a change in mood from "*getting* to . . . *keeping*"—that is, retaining the gains made during the 1930s.[2] They worried that taxes and inflation would erode their incomes—the very issues conservatives would exploit so effectively twenty years later. The more immediate threat, however, was race. Some white workers in the factory districts of Ohio were already nervously eyeing civil rights activism, worried that their jobs would go to black workers; their southern comrades were already astir.

Class and race tensions shook the Democratic party's nominating convention in 1948. Northern liberals, full of fight after their bitter defeat in 1946, went to the convention intent on making war against Taft-Hartley and supporting civil rights. They alienated a large bloc of southern delegates, who formed the States' Rights Democratic party, popularly known as Dixiecrats. With the South Carolinian Strom Thurmond at the head of their ticket, the Dixiecrats campaigned vigorously for states' rights and against integration of public accommodations (Document 2). Although the Democrats won a surprising victory in 1948, Dixiecrats took four southern states. Their showing disclosed what everyone had already suspected: that race was the Achilles' heel of the New Deal coalition in the South.

Race and states' rights continued to haunt the New Deal coalition in the Old South through the 1950s. *Brown v. Board of Education,* the 1954 Supreme Court decision striking down the doctrine of "separate but equal" and mandating integration of public schools, thrust the South into massive resistance. Very few places heeded the Court's decision. Central High School in Little Rock, Arkansas, did not give in until 1957, when President Eisenhower reluctantly ordered a U.S. Army Airborne Division to escort nine black children as they walked to class past screaming picketers.

Northern conservatives like William F. Buckley and *National Review*'s editors (see p. 7) were allied with the South when it came to race. They intoned that the "central question" raised by *Brown* was not one of legality but "whether the white community in the South is entitled to take such measures as are necessary to prevail, politically and culturally, in areas where it does not predominate numerically." The "sobering answer is Yes . . . because it is the advanced race" (Document 7). Buckley later changed his position more than once, but his statement provides a useful glimpse into northern conservative unease and uncertainty about desegregation.

Like racial politics, anticommunist politics also galvanized the fledgling Right. Not long after the onset of the cold war, liberals and conservatives split over the issue of communism. Liberal Democrats and moderate Republicans supported Truman's 1947 program of investigating the political activities of federal employees and requiring them to sign loyalty oaths. In foreign affairs they also signed onto Truman's policy of containing the Soviets in Europe, partly through military alliances but mostly through economic aid. Conservative Republicans, sometimes joined by southern Democrats, called for collapsing the Soviet state and liberating its satellites with military force. They also favored stronger measures against suspected communists in government (Document 3). Senator Joseph McCarthy of Wisconsin held highly publicized Senate subcommittee hearings, during which he grilled known liberals, including members of the Hollywood community, about their alleged communist leanings, costing many their jobs. However, his interrogations began to resemble a circus as he claimed that the communist conspiracy reached beyond the Department of State to the highest echelons of the military.

Although McCarthy was censored for his excesses, he enjoyed great credibility because China was now communist, the Soviets had atomic weapons, and the nation was at war in Korea, its first military operation against communism. General Douglas MacArthur, a much celebrated commander in World War II and head of United Nations forces in Korea, called for a wider war by demanding air strikes against China to punish the communist state for intervening for the Koreans. When, after being reprimanded by the president, the popular general urged a massive invasion of mainland China along with the use of atomic bombs, the president dismissed him. The dismissal made the already popular general a sensation on the Right. Invited to address a joint session of Congress after he was fired, MacArthur spoke wistfully of his military career and closed with the memorable line that he was a mere soldier "who tried to do his duty as God gave him the light to see that duty." Thus, he associated the struggle against communism with God's work, a theme that would resound for years to come. He provided militant anticommunists of the Right with a one-word definition of containment—"appeasement"—and a slogan—"no substitute for victory" (Document 4).

Conservative reactions between 1947 and 1950 to Taft-Hartley, civil rights, and MacArthur were spasmodic outbursts of political sentiment, not the orchestrated voice of a movement. Conservatives had yet to mobilize beyond a few business organizations and veterans' groups. They had only a few journals of marginal importance and no figure of national visibility. All of that began to change in the early 1950s, when a recent graduate of Yale University from a prominent Catholic family burst onto the public stage. Asked to speak at Alumni Day, William F. Buckley fiercely broke with the tradition of celebrating Yale by decrying its departure from "active Christianity" and challenging it to denounce "government paternalism inimical to the dignity of the individual."[3] He would pursue both themes in his 1951 book *God and Man at Yale*, which made the young graduate a right-wing celebrity.

In 1955, after several years of planning, Buckley launched *National Review*, the weekly journal that would become the voice of conservatism for decades. Buckley and his associates envisioned a "highbrow" journal of ideas and opinion similar to the Left's *The Nation* or *The New Republic*; it would not be "a popular or clichéd appeal to the grassroots" (Document 6). The new journal was geared toward fusing three distinct but consonant tendencies of the postwar right: libertarianism, traditionalism, and anticommunism.

Libertarianism, in conservative intellectual eyes, reflected Republicanism's respect for individualism and liberty, which in practical terms boiled down to opposing big government and the redistribution of wealth. Traditionalism looked askance at the individualism of the libertarians and occasionally at modernity itself. More concerned with stability and order, traditionalism harkened to the days when the conventions of faith and deference prevailed and each person knew his or her place. This type of conservatism, sometimes at odds with libertarianism, also had some common ground; for instance, traditionalists were no happier with collectivism (unions, welfare) than were libertarians.

The tensions between libertarianism and traditionalism were held in check and bridged by anticommunism, the single most popular force on the Right and in the nation at large. Although many Americans were anticommunists during the period under examination, conservatives argued that liberalism's toleration for difference and dissent promoted socialism and communism at home and constrained the military abroad.

The leading libertarians of the postwar Right espoused a lofty version of the Republican party's faith in small government, a faith that spread in the aftermath of World War I and deepened in response to the big government programs of the New Deal. In the past it had been associated with Main Street merchants who complained about oppressive regulation and burdensome taxes, but in the 1940s European-trained academics joined their ranks. A leader of this school of thought was Friedrich von Hayek, who spent his early career in Vienna and London before moving to the University of Chicago. Hayek's 1940 classic *The Road to Serfdom* identified robust capitalism (in which private property is organized to maximize private profit) as the mainstay of modern political freedom. It also promoted state policing of the market to prevent companies from forming trusts and reducing their competition.

Milton Friedman, a right-wing thinker who had worked with Hayek at Chicago, inherited Hayek's mantel as the most influential conservative economist. He became a public intellectual in 1980 when his best-selling *Free to Choose* became a television series. That book was a popularized version of his enormously important *Capitalism and Freedom* (1962), in which Friedman argued that freedom was humanity's greatest ideal and government its greatest threat. He advocated a massive shrinkage of government, assailed the income tax as a disincentive to capital accumulation, and urged the privatization of a range of government services, from the postal service to the public schools—proposals that continue to excite conservative imaginations. Perhaps his most important contribution was a critique of Keynesian economics: the liberal notion that government could reduce unemployment in hard times by sponsoring public works funded by taxes raised in good times or by deficit spending. To conservatives, this added up to more government. Friedman proposed the alternative of "monetarism," the idea that changes in the supply of money determine the level of income, the rate of inflation, and the overall pace of economic growth (Document 11).

Not all libertarians were socially conventional. Russian-born Ayn Rand, a rabid anticommunist and foe of both religion and tradition, popularized the idea of individualism in weighty novels that espoused her philosophy of "objectivism," or the "virtue of selfishness," and sold in the millions. More practically, Rand urged a new alliance between businessmen and intellectuals that bore later fruit in the Cato Institute, *Reason* magazine, and other ventures.

Rand's rejection of religion and authority was abhorrent to the traditionalists, whose contempt for egalitarianism and modernism, though often associated with European intellectuals, had an important homegrown advocate. Russell Kirk made his mark with *The Conservative Mind* (1953), an erudite survey of conservative thinkers since the Enlightenment. Kirk's conservatism rested on six basic principles, which included affection for the mystery of religion and traditional life and the necessity of private property and social hierarchy. His disdain for mass society resonated with young conservatives, who were put off by the popular culture of the 1950s, and with today's social conservatives, who want government to uphold "traditional family values" (Document 5).

While Buckley admired Kirk's conservatism, his main commitment, and that of the Right as a whole, was anticommunism. No outlook was more widely shared or evoked such strong emotions, in part because the government was officially anticommunist. Devout Christians and habitual churchgoers thought communism endangered their religion; millions of homeowners saw it as a threat to private property. Moreover, many Americans had friends and family in Eastern European countries that were taken over by communists after World War II. If such immigrants and their children had personal incentives to take a hard line against communism, so did leading conservatives, some of whom were Buckley's close friends and associates—and former communists. For such conservative intellectuals, anticommunism proved to be a powerful brief against liberalism. Liberals could not avoid sounding defensive, almost apologetic, about their squeamishness over McCarthyism and the possibility of nuclear war. The same militant anticommunism that made liberals look soft made conservatives look strong, if sometimes reckless in their willingness to use nuclear weapons.

The tendencies on the Right at this time were promoted by men and women who were aiming to influence mainstream politics. Not all conservatives believed, however, that intellectual influence was enough; they had to support their ideas with action. In that spirit Whittaker Chambers, a former communist turned anticommunist, wrote in 1954 that conservatism had to "accommodate itself to the needs and hopes of the masses—needs and hopes, which like the masses themselves, are the product of machines." He predicted that a conservative movement "that cannot face the facts of the machine and mass production, and its consequences in government and politics, is foredoomed to futility and petulance."[4] He understood earlier and better than most conservative strategists of his generation that conservatism could not succeed without splitting the New Deal coalition. The question was how.

Leading conservatives in the 1950s and 1960s were thinkers, not architects of popular movements. They lacked not only the know-how to build from the ground up but the inclination and temperament as well. Some were dull; others dynamic but miscast. Buckley himself was more comfortable working at his editorial desk or interviewing celebrities on his weekly television show. The closest he came to organizing during this time was when he sponsored the Young Americans for Freedom, the first major youth group on the Right and one that grew fantastically over the next few years, boasting tens of thousands of members by the end of the 1960s. YAF attracted prosperous students on elite campuses and middle-class students, many of them

Catholic, at state universities and Jesuit colleges. Though hardly a mass organization, it was undeniably a start (Document 10).

The most significant organizational breakthrough on the right in this period came from the John Birch Society. The Birchers, who took their name from a Baptist missionary killed by Asian Communists, were the brainchild of Robert Welch, a small businessman and obsessive anticommunist from Massachusetts, who in 1958 organized what would become the nation's most militant anticommunist legion. Although founded in the East, the Birchers were strongest in the West and South, including California, where the movement enjoyed the patronage of wealthy businessmen. In Southern California, the Birchers combined highly charged campaigns against public officials suspected of being soft on communism, with audacious drives to purge libraries of offensive literature and cleanse classrooms of liberal teachers and suspicious curriculums. Welch's conspiratorial view of the world and his habit of making outrageous charges—such as accusing President Eisenhower of being a communist agent—caused even members of Buckley's circle to consider him a kook (Document 8). In 1965 a special edition of *National Review*—in a first for a movement that generally tried at this point to avoid open internal conflict—mocked Welch's theories because they seemed too bizarre and might damage conservative credibility.[5]

In the end, it took a conservative politician, and not an editorialist or journalist, to provide a program for the political right. In 1960, Barry Goldwater, an Arizona senator since 1953, had Buckley's brother-in-law, L. Brent Bozell, ghost-write *The Conscience of a Conservative*. This runaway hit went through twenty printings in two decades, making Goldwater the nation's foremost conservative. He assailed the social programs of the New Deal (including Social Security) and proposed a more militant posture toward the Soviet Union. These beliefs were formulated popularly in Goldwater's slogan "Better dead than red," meaning that it would be better to die from a nuclear attack than to be ruled by communists. Goldwater also exploited white anxiety over racial politics in the South. Integrated schools, he wrote, "were wise and just," but court orders were not the way to achieve them because they violated the nation's cherished states' rights tradition (Document 9).

The Goldwater campaign for the presidency in 1964 showcased a rising star: actor Ronald Reagan. During his televised endorsement of Goldwater, the future governor and president denounced big government, savaged high taxes, and condemned communism (Document 12).

Despite Reagan's oratory talent, Goldwater lost the election in a land-slide to Lyndon Johnson, the former vice president who ascended to the presidency after the assassination of President John Kennedy in 1963. But his campaign was a signal moment in the development of American conservatism. It occurred in the midst of the civil rights movement, which was responsible for both landmark antidiscrimination legislation and for antagonizing normally Democratic white workers in both the North and the South. Goldwater offered a radical departure from the consensual politics of the past. He sharpened differences on foreign and domestic policy, trashed virtually every federal social program, and demanded military victory against the communist insurgents in Vietnam and everywhere else. His strong showing in the Deep South demonstrated the appeal of Republican-style conservatism there. And the campaign brought together an expanded group of right-wing activists who would take the cause to the next level. This included Catholics, who were alarmed not only by communism but also by what they felt to be the moral degeneration of the nation, exemplified by promiscuous sex and abortions (Document 13).

EXPANDING THE BASE: 1968–1980

The dozen years between 1968 and 1980 marked more than the beginnings of Republican ascendancy; they also saw the breakup of the New Deal coalition and the advent of conservative domination of American politics. The demise of the New Deal coalition in electoral terms meant that the South and parts of the Midwest rustbelt shifted from the Democrats to the Republicans, turning the Old Confederacy into the most reliably Republican region in the nation. This historic transformation was fueled partly by white backlash against the civil rights movement and the urban crisis. It was accompanied by another backlash of traditional women aroused at first against the women's movement and then by the proposed Equal Rights Amendment and *Roe v. Wade*, the 1973 Supreme Court decision legalizing abortion.

Anti–civil rights activists and antifeminist campaigners were joined by a growing number of single-issue lobbies that were organized to reduce taxes and defend the right to bear arms. These stirrings coincided with the rightward drift of corporate executives who rebelled against the New Deal as economic slowdown spiraled into stagflation, the combination of high unemployment and high inflation. Such business leaders, together with Sunbelt entrepreneurs long associated with conservatism, would provide a powerful force for tax reform, deregulation (easing regulations on businesses), and privatization (having private businesses perform government functions). They also helped finance the think tanks, political action committees, and other conservative interest groups that shot up in the 1970s. The final component of the conservative movement in this period was a new generation of political operatives skilled at fund-raising and political coordination. Richard Viguerie and Paul Weyrich, the two most noteworthy organizers, would rewrite the rules of the political game.

In the meantime, Governor George Wallace of Alabama posed a further threat to Democrats' hopes for a return to their old hegemony in the South and a boost to the Goldwater Republicans' dreams of conquering the region. Unlike Goldwater, Wallace was a native Southerner who assailed school integration, merging racism and anti-intellectualism in a potent "populist" ("people's") message that resonated with middle- and working-class voters. In 1964 Wallace, after considering a presidential run, deferred to Goldwater, but in 1968 he jumped in on the American Independent Party ticket. He amused crowds in the North and South by railing against the "pointy-headed intellectual morons"—intellectuals and bureaucrats who couldn't "even park a bike straight." Asked by a journalist about the burning issues in the North, he snapped, "By the fall of 1968, the people of Cleveland and Chicago . . . will be so God-damned sick and tired of Federal interference in their schools" that they would "vote for Wallace by the thousands"[6] (Document 14). And so they did. The canny populist garnered nearly 14 percent of the vote, taking five states in the Deep South and running well enough in the North to throw the election to Republican Richard Nixon.

Persistent social turmoil at the end of the 1960s stoked the fires of popular conservatism ignited by Wallace. Antiwar demonstrations on top of urban riots found movement conservatives reinforcing Wallace's cry for law and order; some called for the stronger medicine of capital punishment to keep the peace (Documents 16 and 17). At the turn of the decade, Supreme Court decisions that instituted busing to diversify neighborhood schools filled city streets with angry white defenders of their children's schools. The prospect of parents blocking school doors and stoning school buses pleased no one, least of all conservatives already troubled by disorder. They resolved the dilemma by blaming the courts for the excesses of beleaguered white parents. Prominent political cartoonists added that busing would destroy the schools and ruin the Democratic party as well (Document 19).

Guided by Kevin Phillips's influential primer, *The Emerging Republican Majority*, which demonstrated that a combination of Wallace's and Nixon's votes would dominate the country, the Republicans emulated Wallacism through their "Southern Strategy." Vice President Spiro Agnew, a favorite on the fund-raising circuit with his derisive attacks on "campus radicals" and the "liberal establishment," borrowed heavily from Wallace and allowed his boss to take the softer populist line of vowing to remember the "forgotten people" of the "silent majority" (Documents 15 and 20).

Democrats played into the hands of Nixon's strategists after 1968 by revising procedural rules to ensure greater representation of women and racial minorities in the party, as well as calling for a redistribution of income and an end to the Vietnam War. George McGovern ran a spirited but lonely campaign; the American Federation of Labor–Congress of Industrial Organizations (AFL-CIO), the party's northern mainstay since the mid-1930s, broke precedent by refusing to endorse him. Democrats managed to hold on to Congress, but Nixon chalked up a commanding victory that helped solidify his party's control of the South. With help from the Democrats, the "Southern Strategy" had worked.

Business leaders were more concerned about the ailing economy. The storied prosperity of the postwar era, which had ushered millions of working people and unionists from the squalor of urban tenements to the modest comforts of suburbia and the consumer culture, came to a gradual end. Inflation ticked up, productivity went down, and corporate debt soared. The rising real incomes of the past flattened out and then slipped into decline following the first spike in oil prices in the early 1970s, ending the era of the so-called "affluent worker." Lewis Powell, a corporation lawyer and former head of the American Bar Association, whom Nixon would appoint to the Supreme Court, sounded a new note for the nation's business leaders. In a memo prepared for the Chamber and then widely distributed to corporate America, Powell urged a comprehensive counterattack against the antibusiness rhetoric emanating from college campuses, the media, popular journals, and legislatures (Document 18).

Powell's message appealed to those in the boardrooms. Indeed, corporate heads were already assembling a network of organizations consonant with the conservative climate. One of the first was the Business Round Table, a pressure group formed in 1971 by the CEOs of two hundred leading firms with a new agenda of tax reform and deregulation. The Round Table was the most visible organization in a proliferation of business lobbies and political action committees (PACs), which in a few years far outstripped the number of labor PACs. They proved stronger than labor, as evidenced by the dramatic growth and greater determination of the anti-union National Right to Work Committee.

Business advocacy got help from intellectuals and policy makers, just as Powell had recommended. In 1973, Joseph Coors, the conservative head of the Colorado Brewing Company, and Richard Mellon Scaife, a former Goldwater stalwart and heir to a Pittsburgh banking fortune, established the Heritage Foundation, which provided support for conservative intellectuals and policy makers in the vanguard of the rightward turn in the 1970s. David Koch, son of a founding member of the John Birch Society, heir to an oil and gas fortune, and himself an activist, followed the example of Coors and Mellon in 1977 by founding the Cato Institute. Based in Washington, D.C., like Heritage, Cato was more libertarian and more inclined to support scholars and researchers at leading universities. The other major movement think tanks — the Hoover Institution at Stanford University and the American Enterprise Institute for Public Policy Research (AEI) — were already firmly established but grew rapidly in this period. AEI, a relatively obscure publisher for conservative scholars in the 1950s, became a major intellectual center in the 1970s when its budget grew tenfold to over $10 million, matching the Heritage Foundation. AEI supported forty scholars in residence and many more on campuses. Like other think tanks, AEI attracted donations from conservative businessmen, foundations, and corporations (the Lilly Endowment, Ford, and Reader's Digest, among others), and funded policy studies and journals as well as television shows and radio programs.

The American Enterprise Institute also worked with a group of intellectuals and journalists known as "neoconservatives" or "neocons." The conservative political sociologists Irving Kristol and Nathan Glazer and their allies had begun to distance themselves from the liberalism of the Democratic party in the second half of the 1960s. They were influenced by Harvard professor Daniel Patrick Moynihan, who in 1967 wrote that the civil rights movement had crossed the line from advocating equality of opportunity to favoring preferential treatment.

This was a troubling development for these mainly Jewish intellectuals, who associated quotas with policies that had excluded them from higher education. Tensions over welfare and schools strained and sometimes shattered the historic alliance between Jews and African Americans, and some neoconservatives left the Democrats for the Republicans (Document 22).

This conservative resurgence initially had little impact on federal policy. Because of Democratic control of Congress, President Nixon had to expand the regulatory reach of the federal government. He grudgingly signed the Clean Air Act, one of the most ambitious environmental programs of its kind, and supported the creation of the Environmental Protection Agency and the Occupational Safety and Health Administration. The other branches of government in Washington and in the states were not much friendlier to conservatism. In California two court rulings, in 1967 and 1972, during Ronald Reagan's years as governor, liberalized abortion; in 1973 the Supreme Court followed suit in *Roe v. Wade*. The year before, the Equal Rights Amendment (ERA), a favorite cause of the National Organization for Women (NOW), cleared both houses of Congress and was passed on to the states for ratification. NOW also worked with antigun activists to support restrictions on the sale and use of firearms. Each of these actions prompted conservatives to act.

The National Rifle Association had long been a fairly passive organization that mixed weekend skeet shooters, serious hunters, and conservationists, but its political inactivity ended as antigun groups cropped up in the northern cities and suburbs. In the early 1970s the NRA's Office of Legislative Affairs helped defeat a Michigan petition to outlaw handguns. Following the national elections of 1974, the NRA hired a staff of full-time lobbyists to work in the nation's capital and in the states and started a major fund-raising drive to defray the expenses of political activism (Document 21). This new force against gun control was also the inspiration for a number of auxiliaries, including the Second Amendment Foundation. The NRA, already a player on the Right in the second half of the 1970s, would become more militant and powerful in the early 1990s, leading the charge against President Clinton's proposed ban on assault weapons in 1994 by winning the votes of rural Democrats.

Even before the creation of NOW, Phyllis Schlafly supplied the conservative movement with a woman's voice to counter the feminists. A devout Catholic who helped her husband run a small anticommunist foundation, she shared conservatism's disdain for the Republican party's eastern establishment, a position that informed her ringing endorsement of Barry Goldwater in her 1964 book, *A Choice Not an Echo*. When the party moderates got their revenge by blocking her accession to the head of Federation of Republican Women in 1967, the intrepid conservative rebounded by establishing the Eagle Trust Fund and putting out a monthly newsletter that united the movement's traditionally militant anticommunism with antifeminism.

Schlafly was already calling attention to the alleged dangers of government-subsidized child care when NOW revived the ERA. She formed STOP ERA, a coordinating group that boasted branches in half the states within a year (Document 24). While carefully and deliberately building alliances with Protestant women's groups in the South and West, particularly Mormons and Southern Baptists, Schlafly joined hands with such evangelical activists as Lottie Beth Hobbs, whose antifeminist organization Women Who Want to Be Women would help defeat a child-care bill in the Oklahoma legislature. Schlafly thus helped lay the foundation for the partnership between conservative Catholics and evangelical Protestants that would eventually form the Christian Right.

The task at hand, however, was to defeat the ERA. Thirty states (of thirty-eight needed) had already ratified the amendment when anti-ERA campaigners worked legislative halls, accusing feminists of conspiring to "liberate" women whether they wanted it or not. They warned that churches would lose their tax exemption and that soldiers and firefighters would share foxholes and bunks with women if the ERA passed.[7] In state after state, STOP ERA defeated the amendment, resulting in a banner victory for the conservative movement.

Unlike core antifeminists, the members of the 1970s tax rebellion were not initially associated with the Republican party or the conservative movement but came from all political directions. However, right-wingers, who had long favored low taxes and small government, took the initiative, and conservative Republicans, long hostile to high taxes, soon won over the discontented. While corporations and individuals in 1950 equally shared the national tax bill, tax reforms over the next twenty years shifted the burden to individuals and families, whose combined share of income and Social Security taxes rose to 70 percent of the total. It would swell to nearly 80 percent by the end of the 1970s. State and local taxes ballooned as well, hitting lower- and middle-income families especially hard. Property owners in the suburbs suffered even more because local schools depended on property taxes, which accounted for the lion's share of local levies as the 1960s turned into the 1970s. The stagflation of the 1970s meant something had to give. Howard Jarvis of California, a longtime right-wing activist, made sure that something *did* give by leading the successful campaign to pass Proposition 13. This dramatically lowered property taxes and made it impossible to raise them again, even to pay for police and schools, unless communities explicitly authorized it by popular referendum. Conservatives eagerly enlisted in the tax rebellion, and taxation put wind in Republican sails.

Democrats were stymied. The supposed voice of working people wound up on the wrong side of tax reform now that a good number of Democrats were teachers, sanitation workers, and other public employees dependent on taxes for their programs and livelihoods. Teachers—heavily unionized, socially liberal, and overwhelmingly Democratic—were especially sitting targets (Document 26). Their party ceded substantial political terrain to Republicans, who took the credit for tax relief for working families (Document 23). As more and more people and jobs moved from the North to the South and West, the unions that formed the core of the Democratic party weakened. This demographic shift across regions, together with the general acceleration of suburbanization, increased political representation in the more conservative Sunbelt at the expense of the more liberal Frostbelt (Table 1). The continued flight of industrial jobs from the South to the Third World further complicated Democratic politics, thwarting party liberals' efforts to encourage unionism and protect pensions and other benefits because such policies drove up costs for businesses forced to compete in global markets.

Meanwhile, the battle to move the formerly Democratic South decisively and permanently to the Republicans continued. Few advocates of Sunbelt conservatism left a deeper imprint than Texan Richard Viguerie. Fresh from the Goldwater campaign, he founded his own fund-raising firm, using direct mail to raise money for conservatives in

Table 1. *Apportionment of the House of Representatives, 1950–2000*

REGION	1950	2000	NET CHANGE
Northeast	114	83	−31
South	134	154	+20
Midwest	125	100	−25
West	59	98	+39

Source: "Congressional Apportionment," <http://nationalatlas.gov>.

the 1960s. Viguerie became acquainted with Paul Weyrich, the son of a German Catholic from Wisconsin, who had also stumped for Goldwater and knew Joseph Coors. It was Weyrich who prevailed upon Coors in 1974 to fund the Heritage Foundation, as well as the Committee for the Survival of a Free Congress, a formidable political action committee directed by Weyrich with Viguerie as his fund-raiser. Viguerie's pioneering efforts in direct-mail fund-raising, particularly from ideologically motivated small donors, many of them southern, gave conservatives a twenty-year head start over liberals in raising political money.

Movement conservatives also worked for a more muscular foreign policy, fighting President Carter's 1977 proposal to return the Panama Canal to Panama[8] on policy grounds and as a way to bind the "silent majority" more closely to "the conservative movement."[9] One group that was not silent on foreign policy was the Committee on the Present Danger (CPD), an organization formed in 1976 by longtime Cold War policy makers and neoconservatives dismayed by Carter's emphasis on human rights in foreign policy and apparent softness on the Soviets. The CPD worked to "resurrect a militarized doctrine of containment as the cornerstone of U.S. foreign policy."[10] With help from the Young Americans for Freedom and others, the CPD helped block Carter's SALT II treaty limiting nuclear weapons. It was a foregone conclusion that it would also join the coalition against his proposal on the Panama Canal (Documents 25 and 27).

Viguerie and Weyrich turned their attention to domestic policy, starting with taking steps to change the complexion of the Senate. They persuaded conservatives in New Hampshire, Iowa, and Minnesota to challenge incumbent Democrats, activating local branches of the National Rifle Association, the National Right to Work Committee, and STOP ERA. In a stunning reversal, liberals were defeated in all three states. The Iowa race may well have been determined by anti-abortion social conservatives, organized as "Iowans for Life," who worked the neighborhoods hard against the pro-choice Democratic candidate. Their effort impressed Weyrich, who had tried in the 1978 elections to coordinate the evangelical vote from Washington.

Weyrich and Viguerie formulated a plan for a national organization of evangelicals and proposed it to Reverend Jerry Falwell of Lynchburg, Virginia. Falwell, a Southern Baptist fundamentalist with growing national visibility, eagerly responded to the invitation by helping launch the Moral Majority, a loose, sprawling network of Baptist congregations headed by Bob Billings, a leading advocate of Christian schools (Document 28). Within three years the new organization had affiliates in forty states and a bulging treasury, prompted in part by the Carter administration's temporary revocation of the tax exemption of private schools. This angered white families in the South who were trying to avoid integrated public classrooms. The Moral Majority would become a leading voice in the chorus of religious conservatives for a ban on government-funded abortions and mark the beginnings of a more ecumenical and political Christianity.

Conservative activists in 1974 had despaired at the Watergate scandal that pushed Nixon out of the presidency, fearing that their party was too discredited to survive. They wondered if it was even worth saving, when Vice President Gerald Ford, who replaced Nixon in the White House, chose liberal Republican Nelson Rockefeller to succeed him as vice president. After briefly considering a third party headed by George Wallace, however, Viguerie and Weyrich instead worked on building conservative support during the rest of the decade. In 1980 they teamed up with fellow operatives to unite conservatives into a grand coalition behind Ronald Reagan.

CLEAN SWEEP, 1980–2000

Ronald Reagan was the defining political figure of the conservative movement in the last quarter of the century. A scant two years after his stirring endorsement of Goldwater in 1964, he became governor of California. Reagan soft-pedaled social conservatism but came down hard on urban violence and campus disruption. He reflected the gentler side of economic conservatism, trading the harsh preachiness of free-market zealots for the rhetorical idealism of men like popular theorist George Gilder (Document 30). Reagan promoted smaller government and anticommunism on a global scale and went after the Carter administration on foreign policy, criticizing its passive response to the Soviet invasion of Afghanistan in 1979 and ridiculing its policy of arms control. When Iranian revolutionaries seized the American Embassy in Tehran and took fifty-two American hostages, Carter's botched military rescue six months into the crisis made a confused administration look inept.

Reagan was the Republican party's overwhelming choice for president in 1980. At sixty-six years of age, and thus the oldest presidential nominee ever, Reagan was well financed and characteristically upbeat on the campaign trail against Carter and John Anderson, the moderate

Republican who ran a third-party campaign that hurt Carter. Backed by the political operatives of the conservative movement and the newly formed forces of the Christian Right—despite the fact that Reagan was neither a fundamentalist nor a particularly observant Christian—he deftly exploited popular impatience with the Carter administration's economic and foreign policies. He promised to "get government off our backs," an open-ended formulation that businessmen took to mean deregulation and everyone else interpreted as tax relief.

This was a welcome message to foot soldiers of the tax rebellion everywhere, especially in the moody, politically volatile Rustbelt. Southerners (and blue-collar northerners) equated Reagan's presidency with the end of both the busing of schoolchildren and the use of quotas in hiring to make up for racial discrimination in the workforce. This was Reagan's subtle version of his party's "Southern Strategy," which appealed to the racial preoccupations of the older white South and the economic conservatism of the suburban white South. When Reagan began his postconvention campaign for the presidency in Philadelphia, Mississippi—the scene of the 1964 murder of three civil rights workers—every southerner saw significance in the gesture.

Reagan's coded appeal to the politics of race typified the era. The advances against legal segregation, coupled with the decline of the civil rights movement and George Wallace's retirement, changed the discourse of race from overt appeals to white supremacy to more symbolic gestures. Sometimes a muted form of the old style erupted. Jesse Helms, the former North Carolina banker and radio commentator who combined rabid anticommunism with white supremacy in his popular broadcasts, left the Democratic party for the Republicans in 1970, becoming in 1972 the third Republican (after Thurmond and Texan John Tower) elected to the Senate in the South since Reconstruction. Helms was reelected four times, including after a heated race in 1990 against an African American that featured an advertisement showing a layoff slip handed to a white worker who lost his job because of affirmative action. This kind of symbolic campaigning also cropped up in the presidential race of 1988, which pitted George H. W. Bush against Michael Dukakis, the governor of Massachusetts who had supported weekend furloughs for convicts. The Bush campaign ran an ad showing a revolving door with black criminals exiting jail, while a voice-over asserted that a Dukakis presidency would set free convicted murderers. Race was never far from the minds of Republican office-seekers, moderates as well as conservatives, but they more typically avoided race or adopted Reagan's subtle approach.

And Reagan's strategy proved a smashing success in the 1980 election. Although he garnered only 51 percent of the popular vote, he carried forty-four states and nearly 500 electoral votes on the strength of two trends. About one-third of Carter's supporters in the North and South deserted him for Reagan, earning them the handle of "Reagan Democrats." Another large group of Democrats stayed home, abstaining rather than voting for an incumbent who had lost their confidence or a Republican who was too far to the right. Voter turnout sank to 53 percent of the eligible electorate, the lowest number since 1920.[11]

The popular vote, while just barely behind Reagan, emphatically tilted the House to the right by electing thirty-three Republicans, most of them in the South. They did even better in the Senate, defeating twelve of fourteen incumbents targeted by movement conservatives and taking control of the Senate for the first time since 1954. The Christian Right, which was still in formation and not quite the force it would later become in national politics, often made the critical difference in statewide elections. Jerry Falwell's followers in the Moral Majority targeted forty-three representatives and senators for insufficient Christian morality, singling out high-profile members in the Midwest. In Oklahoma Betty Grogan and her daughter, Sandra Grogan Jeter, who were members of the Church of Christ and recruits in Phyllis Schlafly's antifeminist crusade, reported that they had knocked on over 3,000 doors and helped carry the state not only for Reagan but also for first-time Senator Don Nickles, who quickly rose to become majority leader of his party. Untold numbers of other men and women associated with the Christian Right and the single-issue political action committees followed the Grogans' example.

The new president acted swiftly to put his stamp on the presidency, inaugurating what came to be called the "Reagan Revolution." In an acceptance speech brimming with optimism and filled with references to the nation's more heroic moments, the "Great Communicator" held Democrats responsible for the "malaise" born of economic stagnation and the humiliation of the Iran hostage crisis. Reagan promised steep tax cuts and a mightier military, but he spoke mostly of a renewed spirit, ironically borrowing the line from no less than Franklin Delano Roosevelt that the nation had (another) "rendezvous with destiny" (Document 29).

Two dramatic episodes proved pivotal moments in the early Reagan years: the strike of the Professional Air Traffic Controllers' Organization (PATCO) and the invasion of Grenada. In 1981 air traffic controllers struck for higher wages and better working conditions, despite a federal ban on strikes by federal employees. The president immediately ordered the strikers back to work on pain of dismissal; over 11,000 were fired and banned from government employment for life. Two years later the president ordered Marines into Grenada on the grounds that the newly elected left-wing government of the small Caribbean island was a staging area of the Soviets. In between these bold assertions of presidential power, Reagan scored the most important legislative victories of his first term. First came tax cuts, the favorite cause of conservatives and pushed hard by Reagan staffers who embraced the theory of "supply-side economics." They believed that major tax cuts for the rich would not only free up capital for investment but would also increase tax revenues because of an expected surge in growth. Congress next approved the president's Economy Recovery Tax Act, which cut tax rates 25 percent, with accelerated depreciation allowances and tax credits for businesses. It then imposed steep reductions in spending over five years on programs for the poor and needy—food stamps, unemployment insurance, and welfare benefits—of the kind George Gilder and others had long endorsed (Document 30).

The new administration also pursued a vigorous policy of deregulation (Document 36). The president froze new regulations by executive order and ordered a massive rollback of existing rules, including limits on radio commercials and controls on the production and allocation of oil. He brought to heel federal agencies responsible for monitoring air and water pollution and for enforcing labor laws, replacing carryovers from the Nixon and Carter administrations with more conservative appointees fresh from posts with the right-wing think tanks, especially Heritage. In a sign of the times, the former legal counsel of the National Right to Work Committee became the chief counsel of the National Labor Relations Board, the agency that would, among other things, supervise unionization votes.

Conservative intellectuals and policy advocates were disappointed by Reagan's attack on federal regulation and public services. They wanted a thorough house cleaning along the lines laid out in the Heritage Foundation's 3,000-page report, *Mandate for Leadership*, which recommended eliminating the Departments of Education and Energy and privatizing Social Security, a proposal promoted by libertarians for twenty-five years (Document 32). The president went no farther on privatization than appointing a study commission in the twilight of his second term in 1987, a move that gave the Heritage Foundation and their friends at the Cato Institute another chance to be heard. Their

1988 report, which pushed school vouchers for the poor as well as privatizing Social Security and public housing, was a more accurate gauge of conservative opinion than public policy in Washington (Document 34). Privatization made more headway in the states.

Reagan also reshaped the judiciary into a more conservative mold. He made scores of appointments to the federal bench and three appointments to the Supreme Court, one in his first term (Sandra Day O'Connor) and two in his second (Antonin Scalia and Anthony Kennedy). He also elevated Associate Justice William Rehnquist to Chief Justice. Kennedy was a substitute for Reagan's first choice, Robert Bork, a staunch conservative whose nomination was defeated in the Senate by an alliance of Democrats and moderate Republicans. The group was led by Massachusetts Senator Edward Kennedy, who charged that Bork would force women into "back-alley abortions" and African Americans to "segregated lunch counters."[12] The pyrotechnics produced the verb *Borking*, which *The New York Times* defined as "to destroy a judicial nominee through a concerted attack on his character."[13] It provided the conservative movement with a grievance and a wrong it would attempt to avenge in future battles over the Court.

Even without Bork the Supreme Court bent to the right, if not as far as some conservatives would have liked. O'Connor and Kennedy became swing votes in cases involving the hot-button issues of affirmative action, abortion, and the right to privacy, joining three moderates on the common legal platform of respecting settled law through the doctrine of *stare decisis*. Rehnquist and Scalia, soon to be joined by George H. W. Bush appointee Clarence Thomas, formed the hard right of the Court, rejecting *stare decisis* in favor of the strict constructionist doctrines of "textualism" and "original intent," which looked past legal precedent to the Constitution and its framers in 1787. That doctrine informed their opposition to gun control and the right to privacy as well as their support for the death penalty (Document 35).

Neoconservatives, many of whom were active in the Committee on the Present Danger (CPD) and formerly in residence at the American Enterprise Institute, also landed key positions during the Reagan administration. They were behind the president's massive buildup in the nation's military capacity. This dazzling investment of over $1 trillion included high-technology weaponry shelved during the Carter years and such new programs as the Strategic Defense Initiative ("Star Wars") that envisioned a network of satellites that would shoot down missiles headed for the United States. Reagan had it both ways on the Soviet Union: He took a hard line by calling it the "evil empire" and demanding that Soviet leader Mikhail Gorbachev "tear down" the Berlin Wall, but he also sat down with Gorbachev to negotiate cultural exchanges and arms reduction. When the USSR collapsed in 1991, Reagan got the credit for having won the cold war.

The one faction of the conservative movement that did not fare well in the Reagan years was the Christian Right. In 1982 the administration imposed a rule prohibiting the distribution of contraceptives to minors without parental consent. A year later Reagan assailed critics of his abortion policy and the defenders of *Roe v. Wade* in a much-publicized address to the National Association of Evangelicals, an umbrella group of Protestant ministers and lay activists (Document 31). But the president never went much beyond lip service to the Christian Right. Scholars and pundits still wonder why. The administration seemed simply to place greater priority on tax cuts and deregulation and on confronting communism on a global scale.

The Christian Right itself was still in its infancy. It shared the anti-modernist ethos of the traditionalist wing of the New Right but was more popular than the traditionalists and very much a newcomer to the Republican party. Evangelicals had once inhabited the conservative wing of the New Deal coalition, if largely because of Southern allegiances; as late as the 1980s they divided evenly between the parties. Social conservatives could count on the Church of Jesus Christ of Latter-day Saints and the Lutheran-Church Missouri Synod and on the Catholic Church, the leading religious denominations opposing the right to abortion. Both the Lutherans and the Mormons, however, were concentrated in a few states. The political alliance of the churches in the 1980s was therefore more effective at the local level in certain states in the Midwest, far West, and South. Moreover, not all sects, even in the South, were on board about abortion. The Southern Baptist Convention (SBC), the largest Protestant denomination in the nation, had long observed fundamentalism's literal interpretation of biblical strictures against dance, drink, and premarital sex. But it was never very political or in step with Catholics and other denominations on abortion or gay rights. Its pronouncements through the 1970s on abortion allowed exceptions for the mental and physical health of the mother. But the church toughened its position in 1979 and again in 1984, declaring abortion to be a form of "murder" and impermissible under any circumstances (Document 33). Denominations like the SBC had no difficulty communing with fellow Baptist Jerry Falwell, but Falwell himself never fully overcame evangelicalism's historic suspicion of Catholicism—or other denominations of Protestantism. The Moral

Majority continued to be narrowly tied to his Bible Baptists for the most part, and in the late 1980s Falwell folded the organization.

The Christian Right found unity at the end of the 1980s due to the influence of politicized clergy and Republican lay activists who pushed the church farther rightward and linked it more firmly to the party. Reverend Tim and Beverly LaHaye were closely aligned with the Moral Majority through Tim's membership on its board and Beverly's Concerned Women for America (CWA), which had worked with Schlafly's Eagle Forum against the Equal Rights Amendment. CWA prospered in the 1980s and into the 1990s, by which point the LaHayes shifted focus from political activism to media work, including Beverly's popular radio show, *Bev LaHaye Live.* Tim concentrated on his wildly popular series of books, *Left Behind,* all driven by the theme of the "rapture" in which Christ returns to earth to save the faithful, leaving the others behind to gruesome fates.

One of the prominent new faces on the Christian Right was James Dobson, a Southern California family therapist. In 1977 he formed Focus on the Family (FF), a family therapy group supported by AMWAY and other conservative businesses. Dobson echoed the rightward turn within Sunbelt Protestantism in the late 1980s, persuading the board of FF to restate its mission so that it would "cooperate with the Holy Spirit in disseminating the Gospel of Jesus Christ to as many people as possible and, specifically, to accomplish that objective by helping to preserve traditional family values and the institution of the family."[14] Four years later, in 1992, he separated Focus on the Family from his Family Research Council (FRC) and put FRC in the hands of Gary Bauer. A former official in Reagan's Department of Education, Bauer in less than a decade made FRC one of the wealthiest, most effective voices of the Christian Right. He drew support from conservative foundations and businesses, built support in the states, and worked out alliances with sympathetic denominations and lay groups.

The Christian Right, now much stronger at the grassroots level in the states, gained another national voice in Reverend Pat Robertson, a Portsmouth, Virginia, minister. Robertson suddenly announced in 1986 that he would make a run at the presidency in 1988, only to see his campaign fizzle. He then shifted gears by forming the Christian Coalition to replace the defunct Moral Majority. Robertson closely followed the script being written in the evangelical churches by looking to the political arena for leadership. He tapped Ralph Reed, head of the College Republicans and a newly converted fundamentalist, to direct the Christian Coalition. Within a year Reed had a big budget, a publication (*Christian America*), and a comprehensive plan to take advantage of politically charged grassroots lobbies in the Sunbelt. Reed perfected the art developed decades earlier by states' rights southerners and the Birchers of portraying the Right as a persecuted minority victimized by liberals and secular humanists. It worked very well. Reed linked up with activists in Virginia and Florida to fight sex education programs in the schools and defeat a gay rights proposal. In 1991 he presented 50,000 Christian Coalition petitions to the Senate in support of the nomination of Clarence Thomas to the Supreme Court.

As the Christian Right grew in power and size, it also became more ecumenical. The tenuous, sometimes troubled alliance between Catholic conservatives and Protestant evangelicals matured at the end of the 1980s into a more reliable partnership on moral issues. The influx of immigrants from Third World countries, hostile to gay rights and abortion, nudged Catholicism rightward. So did the appointment by Pope John Paul II of conservative bishops unfriendly to the social justice ethos of Vatican II, the conclave of Catholic prelates that met from 1962 to 1965 to reform the liturgy and relax the dogma. Lay activists worked to unite Catholics and Protestants around a program of making religious conservatism a public issue. They formed Evangelicals and Catholics Together (ECT), which issued manifestos endorsed by conservative clerics; one referred to them as evidence of "the end of the Reformation."[15] This was an aggressive ecumenicalism—what one loyalist called a "co-belligerency"—of Catholic and Protestant around "family values" that reached from lectern to pulpit (Documents 37 and 39). Co-belligerents in the 1990s chalked up a string of state victories that included waiting periods for abortion and exempting gays from civil rights protections.

The Christian Right got little cooperation from President George H. W. Bush, Reagan's former vice president, and even less from Democrat Bill Clinton, who won in 1992 largely because third-party candidate Ross Perot split the Republican vote. Christian Right activists had their doubts about Clinton confirmed when he signed a bill providing unpaid leave from work for new parents and tried to lift the ban on gays in the military. Journalists linked to the Christian Right and long-time movement backers such as Richard Mellon Scaife funded a sustained and far-reaching smear campaign against Clinton and his wife Hillary. Wild charges flew long before the failed attempt in 1998 to impeach the president. The embattled chief executive was charged with everything from shady land deals to having extramarital affairs. Extreme Clinton haters charged him with arranging the murder of a political aide.

Such scandal provided copy for the "shock jocks," a new breed of radio commentator who had pierced the din of Motown and country music on AM radio since the 1980s. Rush Limbaugh had a gift for mixing irreverence (he called Chelsea Clinton, the Clintons' daughter, the "White House dog") with a sharp-edged populism charged with the pieties of the Christian Right and an obsessive disdain for the Clintons and liberalism. He had hundreds of imitators by the 1990s, some of whom enjoyed national exposure in part because of the consolidation of the major broadcasting systems by conservative businessmen. Limbaugh left it to others, however, to move the chronic liberal bashing from radio to print. Ann Coulter became one of the most incendiary, publishing several books in quick succession with such one-liners as "Even Islamic terrorists don't hate America like liberals do."[16]

The free-market message of David Frum, a Canadian-born journalist and political speechwriter, was similar to that of Ayn Rand. Frum sought to promote personal responsibility and social order despite the lingering vestiges of the New Deal. He attributed crime, single parenthood, and laziness to the "seductive invitation to misconduct" of the welfare state, which insulated the poor and the young from the discipline and rigors of the capitalist marketplace and suggested to Frum that the much-heralded Reagan Revolution was a misnomer. It had left too much of the New Deal untouched and too many Americans unchanged (Document 38).

The publication of Frum's book *Dead Right* coincided with what many Movement operatives thought was another chance to complete the Reagan Revolution, this time under a new command. Seven months before the fall 1994 elections, Georgia Representative Newt Gingrich drafted "The Contract with America," a conservative manifesto calling for constitutional amendments mandating a balanced budget and term limits for congressional officerholders along with tax cuts, entitlement restrictions, and regulatory rollbacks. It also aimed to purge Washington of scandal and corruption.

The Contract was not uniformly popular with movement conservatives. It ignored such "traditional family values" issues as abortion and gay rights, reflecting the deep factional tensions that continued to frustrate the movement. Such issues made Gingrich fear the alienation of the party's economic conservatives and small government advocates. Nor were promoters of the flat tax pleased. The flat tax was a hobby horse of libertarians in the conservative think tanks who saw the graduated income tax as the life blood of the New Deal and the Great Society. The flat tax was their dietary pill for the welfare state— a prescription, one said, that would make it possible to "drown [the government] in the bathtub."[17] Randy Tate, a Gingrich associate and former representative from Washington who succeeded Ralph Reed at the Christian Coalition, used the platform of the largest Christian lobby in the nation to claim that the flat tax would increase the incomes of ordinary people and stay "the greedy hand of government." His position demonstrated the resiliency of the tax revolt, as well as the integration of economic with social conservatism under the banner of the conservative movement (Document 40).

Gingrich's gamble in 1994 that the social conservatives of the Christian Right would have no other place to go was correct. A conservative earthquake shook Congress in the November elections. Republicans gained fifty-two seats in the House and ten in the Senate, taking control of Congress for the first time in forty years; it was the greatest electoral triumph for conservatives since 1980. But it was something of a letdown from a policy perspective. GOP lawmakers over the next two years had little to show for their new strength other than forcing the president to sign a welfare reform bill that sharply curtailed cash payments for poor children and required adults to find employment within two years or lose their assistance. Gingrich's tirades discredited him in the eyes of the public and his own party. Clinton was reelected in 1996, thanks largely to a booming economy, but the Republican Right strengthened its hand in Congress.

In the 2000 election, Clinton's vice president, Al Gore, the son of former Democratic Senator Albert Gore, found himself facing another political heir: George W. Bush, the former Texas governor and son of George Herbert Walker Bush. Gore's great advantage was the Clinton boom and a decade of peace, which had piled up millions of jobs and turned the huge deficit inherited from the first Bush administration into a huge surplus. But Gore was an inconsistent and bland campaigner, and he also had to contend with a challenge to his left from Ralph Nader, the candidate of the Green party. Bush offered a stark contrast to Gore's moderation, bringing together the various tendencies on the Right into a comprehensive whole. He promised economic conservatives tax cuts, privatization, and a regulatory reform plan to privatize Social Security, the enduring metaphor for the New Deal. He told Christian conservatives that he opposed abortion and favored government vouchers for tuition at private schools. He pledged to name Supreme Court justices who would line up with Scalia and Thomas, making a conservative majority that would strike down *Roe v. Wade*. No Republican presidential nominee, not Ronald Reagan or Bush's own father, more fully embraced the social conservatism of the Christian Right (Document 42).

The Christian Right in 2000 finally had one of their own at the head of the Republican ticket, an unambiguous champion they could support with conviction and enthusiasm. Older stalwarts Jerry Falwell and Pat Robertson, along with allies such as Ralph Reed and James Dobson, mobilized evangelical Christians through their broadcast outlets and voter guides. Catholic prelates encouraged votes for Bush on their own or teamed up with Protestant co-belligerents. Lay Catholics distributed guides urging voters to assess candidates on abortion, gay marriage, and euthanasia, as well as stem-cell research, one of the new fronts in the culture wars. These groups were joined by the usual business PACs and single-issue lobbies like the NRA. Neoconservatives endorsed Bush, believing he would reject Clinton's policy of nation building and cooperation with the United Nations. They preferred unilateral preemption against foreign enemies and rogue states and were joined by factions of evangelicals led by Tim LaHaye and Pat Robertson, who considered the United Nations an anti-American anti-Christ that would foist upon the people the abomination of "Global Government" (Document 41). Such a broad coalition, armed with a great war chest, made the GOP look like a sure and easy winner.

Nonetheless, the presidential election of 2000 was surprisingly competitive. As predicted, Nader siphoned off a number of liberal votes from Gore. Television networks declared Gore the winner in the state of Florida before the polls closed, but then had to offer a red-faced retraction. The race was too close to call there and, because Gore had a twenty-vote lead in the electoral college without Florida, still undecided nationally. Both sides went to court to resolve the impasse. A recount that seemed to be going Gore's way was stopped by a 5 to 4 decision of the U.S. Supreme Court. The next day Gore conceded the election to Bush, starting a new chapter in the book of American conservatism.

Conservatism decisively shifted the nation's center of political gravity to the right. Politics increasingly played out within a framework constructed by the conservative movement, just as politics in the 1950s still operated within the framework constructed by the New Deal coalition. In January 1996 President Clinton effectively cried "uncle" with his renunciation of "big government," but his party had already conceded much to Republicanism. The Right took over major regulatory bodies, further shifted the tax burden from corporations to families and individuals, and scuttled efforts to make national health insurance part of Social Security. Right-wing activism defeated the Equal Rights Amendment, weakened antigun laws in the states and civil rights statutes in Washington, compromised the right to abortion, thwarted gay marriages, and revived the death penalty. Conservatives grew to dominate the federal judiciary and the foreign policy establishment. The Christian Right moved religion from the privacy of the pew and confessional to the public square, making faith an important part of the national dialogue and elevating faith-based charities to important players in the delivery of human services. A network of corporate executives, right-wing foundations, think tanks, and media outlets kept the pot boiling and the coalition on message. The South was once again solid—but for the Republicans. As of 2000 the Republican party was, it might be said, the conservative movement in action.

NOTES

[1]In November 1979 student activists allied with Iran's new Islamist regime held sixty-six U.S. diplomats and citizens hostage for more than a month; they were released in January 1980.

[2]Samuel Lubell, *The Future of American Politics* (rev. ed., 1955, New York: Doubleday, 1952), 209.

[3]Godfrey Hodgson, *The World Turned Right Side Up: A History of Conservative Ascendancy in America* (Boston: Houghton Mifflin, 1996), 75.

[4]William F. Buckley, ed., *Odyssey of a Friend: Whittaker Chambers' Letters to William F. Buckley, Jr.* (New York: G. P. Putnam's Sons, 1956), 79.

[5]*National Review*, Oct. 19, 1965: 914–20 and 925–29. Also, George H. Nash, *The Conservative Intellectual Movement in America since 1945* (New York: Basic Books, 1945), 292–93.

[6]Quoted in John Mickelthwait and Adrian Wooldridge, *The Right Nation: Conservative Power in America* (New York: Penguin, 2004), 66.

[7]Ruth Murray Brown, *"For a Christian America": A History of the Religious Right* (Amherst, N.Y.: Prometheus Books, 2002), 39–43, 90.

[8]Following a failed attempt by the French, the Panama Canal was built in the early twentieth century by the United States. The land for it (the "Canal Zone") was given to the United States by the government of Panama in return for U.S. support in its independence struggle against Colombia. The Carter administration decided to return the canal to Panama for strategic reasons.

[9]Richard A. Viguerie, *The New Right: We're Ready to Lead* (rev. ed. 1981, Falls Church, Va.: The Viguerie Company, 1980), 65.

[10]Quoted in Sara Diamond, *Roads to Dominion: Right-Wing Movements and Political Power in the United States* (New York: Guilford, 1995), 195–96.

[11] Fred Siegel, *Troubled Journey: From Pearl Harbor to Ronald Reagan* (New York: Hill & Wang, 1984), 269.

[12] Robert Bork, <www.wikipedia.org>.

[13] Ibid.

[14] Quoted in Brown, "*For a Christian America*," 175.

[15] Garry Wills, "Fringe Government," *New York Review of Books*, 52 (Oct. 6, 2005): 46–50.

[16] Quoted in Mickelthwait and Wooldridge, *Right Nation*, 287.

[17] Norquist, <www.wikipedia.org>.

PART TWO

The Documents

1

First Steps, 1945–1968

1

DAVID LAWRENCE

America Turns the Corner

July 11, 1947

By 1945 union members numbered 15 million, a figure that appalled most conservatives. Corporations complained about higher labor costs, traditionalists about collectivist threats to self-reliance, and Republicans about unions as a Democratic bulwark that sustained the policies of the New Deal. And labor, already strong in the industrial North, seemed poised to invade the anti-union South.

In 1947 conservatives celebrated their first victory: passage, over Harry Truman's veto, of the Taft-Hartley Labor Management Relations Act. The Act made it harder to establish a "union shop," in which a company's new workers are required to join a union; prohibited unions from making campaign contributions; barred secondary boycotts or sympathy strikes; permitted the president to delay strikes that endangered the country's health or security; and sanctioned "right to work laws" in the states. As a result, unions failed to organize the South and eventually, after tougher congressional acts and unremitting conservative opposition, slowly lost political clout. In this sense the Act was the first conservative victory in the long campaign to reverse the liberal tide of the twentieth century.

The architect of the Act was Senator Robert Taft—"Mr. Republican"—renowned for his isolationism and opposition to the New Deal.

David Lawrence, "America Turns the Corner," *The United States News*, July 11, 1947.

Beaten by Eisenhower for the Republican presidential nomination in 1952, Taft died the next year, leaving Taft-Hartley as his legacy. David Lawrence was the publisher of The United States News, *which would eventually form the core of* U.S. News and World Report, *the country's most consistently and thoroughly conservative newsweekly.*

June 1947 was an epochal month in American history. . . .

It marked the overthrow of socialistic government in the United States. This occurred when the Democratic and Republican parties assembled a two-thirds vote in both houses of Congress to override a presidential veto and put an end to what has been for nearly 14 years a government controlled in all its branches by national labor unions.

The vote to enact the Taft-Hartley bill was significant entirely apart from the fact that the Wagner labor relations law of 1935 [which gave workers the right to try to organize unions] was rewritten and a balanced measure, fair to management and unions alike, substituted.

Most significant was the vote of two thirds of both houses to turn back those forces of special privilege which had sought to set up in America a supergovernment directed and controlled by labor unions and operated under the protection of a one-sided collective bargaining law.

Boldly challenging the political power of the labor unions by insisting that there must be no misuse of union members' dues for political purposes, the new statute proclaims a doctrine of liberalism which is traditional in our country—a doctrine which says that excessive sums of money spent without the consent of stockholders in corporations or members of unions shall not influence the outcome of elections for the presidency and for members of Congress. If these abuses had not been checked, representative government in America could have been destroyed by minority groups. . . .

As long as 100 Democrats from the Solid South and border states and a minimum of 118 Republicans—out of the present strength of 245—are elected from the North, the House of Representatives will possess an anti-radical majority for years to come. This can block any repeal of the Taft-Hartley law or any return to "left wing" policies. Neither the election of a Democratic President in 1948 nor the election of a Democratic House or Senate can alter the fact that the veto power has shifted from the White House to the House of Representatives. There the anti-radical votes of both Republican and Democratic parties—constituting the people's veto—are sufficient to prevent radicalism from gaining power again over the purse strings of government or over the jobs of individual citizens.

America, therefore, has turned the corner—has turned from more than a decade of loose, arbitrary and capricious handling of public funds and public power to a new era. It will be an era of relative stability because at least the finances of the United States will be on a sound basis and our whole system of productive enterprise no longer will be threatened by a handful of national labor-union leaders anxious only to perpetuate their own oligarchy and to dominate the Federal Government....

It took a firm hand to steer the nation through the economic pitfalls of the period that followed the War Between the States in the second half of the last century.

It took a firm hand to steer the nation through the reconstruction period that followed World War I when the debt was reduced and the tax burden was steadily diminished.

It has taken a firm hand to get rid of the New Deal, which was really on the way out in 1940 after seven years of unprecedented deficits in our yearly budgets. It was only the outbreak of total war in 1940 that accidentally gave the New Deal government another lease on life for nearly six years. In 1946 the congressional elections belatedly expressed the people's determination to put an end to radicalism in the Federal Government.

America has turned away from state socialism, wherein the government is the master and the citizen is the servant.

America has turned again to the truly representative system where government is the servant and the whole people are once more masters of their own destiny.

2

STROM THURMOND ET AL.

Platform of the States' Rights Democratic Party
1948

The former Confederate slave states had long been a Democratic bastion committed to the preservation of white supremacy. But the times and the party were changing. Franklin Roosevelt established procedures to contest discriminatory hiring, and his wife, Eleanor, appeared openly in public with black leaders. Federal courts ordered the desegregation of some southern law schools; the GI Bill provided benefits for both black and white veterans. Harry Truman desegregated the army and proposed a package outlawing lynching, segregation, and the poll tax.* The 1948 Democratic convention, over angry southern objections, endorsed his proposals and applauded Minnesotan Hubert Humphrey, who urged the convention to "get out of the shadow of states' rights."

Disaffected southern Democrats formed the States' Rights Democratic Party, or "Dixiecrats," which carried four Deep South states in 1948 and shattered the "Solid South." Its leader, Strom Thurmond of South Carolina, would become a symbol of states' rights and racial conservatism, draft a "Southern Manifesto" attacking school desegregation, and mount a record twenty-four-hour filibuster against a 1957 civil rights bill. Thurmond showed that the race issue could put the South in political play. He never endorsed a Democratic presidential candidate after 1944, and in 1964 switched to the Republican party.

---

*Poll taxes typically took the form of a $2.00 levy per person in order to vote. Although they were sometimes used earlier in many states, poll taxes were commonly imposed in the South during the 1890s to prohibit voting by African Americans, who were too poor to pay and thus could not vote. Poll taxes and similar instruments designed to discourage voting were banned in 1964 by the Twenty-fourth Amendment to the Constitution.

Strom Thurmond et al., "Platform of the States' Rights Democratic Party." In Arthur M. Schlesinger Jr., ed., *History of U.S. Political Parties, Volume IV, 1945–1972: The Politics of Change* (New York: Chelsea House Publishers, 1973), 3422–25.

1. We believe that the Constitution of the United States is the greatest charter of human liberty ever conceived by the mind of man.
2. We oppose all efforts to invade or destroy the rights guaranteed by it to every citizen of this republic.
3. We stand for social and economic justice, which we believe can be guaranteed to all citizens only by a strict adherence to our Constitution and the avoidance of any invasion or destruction of the constitutional rights of the states and individuals. We oppose the totalitarian, centralized bureaucratic government and the police nation called for by the platforms adopted by the Democratic and Republican Conventions.
4. We stand for the segregation of the races and the racial integrity of each race; the constitutional right to choose one's associates; to accept private employment without governmental interference, and to earn one's living in any lawful way. We oppose the elimination of segregation, the repeal of miscegenation statutes, the control of private employment by Federal bureaucrats called for by the misnamed civil rights program. We favor home-rule, local self-government and a minimum interference with individual rights.
5. We oppose and condemn the action of the Democratic Convention in sponsoring a civil rights program calling for the elimination of segregation, social equality by Federal fiat regulations of private employment practices, voting, and local law enforcement.
6. We affirm that the effective enforcement of such a program would be utterly destructive of the social, economic and political life of the Southern people, and of other localities in which there may be differences in race, creed or national origin in appreciable numbers.
7. We stand for the check and balances provided by the three departments of our government. We oppose the usurpation of legislative functions by the executive and judicial departments. We unreservedly condemn the effort to establish in the United States a police nation that would destroy the last vestige of liberty enjoyed by a citizen.
8. We demand that there be returned to the people to whom of right they belong, those powers needed for the preservation of human rights and the discharge of our responsibility as

democrats for human welfare. We oppose a denial of those by
political parties, a barter or sale of those rights by a political
convention, as well as any invasion or violation of those rights
by the Federal Government. We call upon all Democrats and
upon all other loyal Americans who are opposed to totalitarianism at home and abroad to unite with us in ignominiously
defeating Harry S. Truman, Thomas E. Dewey, and every
other candidate for public office who would establish a Police
Nation in the United States of America.

9. We, therefore, urge that this Convention endorse the candi-
dacies of J. Strom Thurmond and Fielding H. Wright for the
President and Vice-President, respectively, of the United
States of America.

3

JOSEPH R. McCARTHY

Lincoln Day Address
February 20, 1950

*By 1950 a world that seemed brighter after the end of World War II was
filled with ominous signs: Eastern Europe lost behind an ideological
"iron curtain," the Soviets with atomic weapons, Communists victorious
in China, anticolonial revolutions raging. How did this happen? Wisconsin Senator Joseph McCarthy believed he knew the answer. The Roosevelt-
Truman administrations harbored traitors and subversives, men who
were at the very least Communist dupes and sympathizers, if not Communists themselves. "Comsymps" were not easy to discern because they
hid their true identities and looked like everybody else. McCarthy con-
vened his Internal Security Subcommittee to ferret them out.*

*McCarthy ultimately discredited himself when he accused military
officers and, by implication, President Eisenhower of conspiracy. The
Senate censured him in 1954 by a 2 to 1 margin; by 1957 McCarthy*

Joseph R. McCarthy, "Lincoln Day Address," *Congressional Record* (February 20, 1950).

was dead. For a time, however, he was supported by huge swaths of the public, including conservatives such as William F. Buckley, who defended McCarthy's rough tactics and goals as essential to rolling back world communism and domestic "collectivism" (labor unions, high taxes, government programs). His chief legacy was "McCarthyism"—the equation of liberalism with socialism with communism with subversion, and the linking of foreign failure with criticism of domestic policies and subversion. He also undermined the Democrats' stature as mighty wartime leaders, a reputation they never entirely recovered.

Today we are engaged in a final, all-out battle between Communistic atheism and Christianity. The modern champions of Communism have selected this as the time. And, ladies and gentlemen, the chips are down—they are truly down.

Six years ago, at the time of the first conference to map out the peace . . . there was within the Soviet orbit 180 million people. Lined up on the antitotalitarian side there were in the world roughly 1,625 million people. Today, only six years later, there are 800 million people under the absolute domination of Soviet Russia—an increase of over 400 percent. On our side, the figure has shrunk to around 500 million. In other words, in less than six years the odds have changed from 9 to 1 in our favor to 8 to 5 against us. This indicates the swiftness of the tempo of Communist victories and American defeats in the cold war. As one of our outstanding historical figures once said, "When a great democracy is destroyed, it will not be because of enemies from without, but rather because of enemies from within."

The truth of this statement is becoming terrifyingly clear as we see this country each day losing on every front. . . .

The reason why we find ourselves in a position of impotency is not because our only powerful potential enemy has sent men to invade our shores, but rather because of the traitorous actions of those who have been treated so well by this Nation. It has not been the less fortunate or members of minority groups who have been selling this Nation out, but rather those who have had all the benefits that the wealthiest nation on earth has had to offer—the finest homes, the finest college education, and the finest jobs in Government we can give.

This is glaringly true in the State Department. There the bright young men who are born with silver spoons in their mouths are the ones who have been worst. . . . In my opinion the State Department, which is one of the most important government departments, is thoroughly infested with Communists.

I have in my hand 57 cases of individuals who would appear to be either card carrying members or certainly loyal to the Communist Party, but who nevertheless are still helping to shape our foreign policy.

One thing to remember in discussing the Communists in our Government is that we are not dealing with spies who get 30 pieces of silver to steal the blueprints of a new weapon. We are dealing with a far more sinister type of activity because it permits the enemy to guide and shape our policy. . . .

As you hear this story of high treason, I know that you are saying to yourself, "Well, why doesn't the Congress do something about it?" Actually, ladies and gentlemen, one of the important reasons for the graft, the corruption, the dishonesty, the disloyalty, the treason in high Government positions—one of the most important reasons why this continues is a lack of moral uprising on the part of the 140 million American people. In the light of history, however, this is not hard to explain.

It is the result of an emotional hangover and a temporary moral lapse which follows every war. It is the apathy to evil which people who have been subjected to the tremendous evils of war feel. As the people of the world see mass murder, the destruction of defenseless and innocent people, and all of the crime and lack of morals which go with war, they become numb and apathetic. It has always been thus after war.

However, the morals of our people have not been destroyed. They still exist. This cloak of numbness and apathy has only needed a spark to rekindle them. Happily, this spark has finally been supplied.

As you know, very recently the Secretary of State [Dean Acheson] proclaimed his loyalty to a man [Alger Hiss] guilty of what has always been considered as the most abominable of all crimes—of being a traitor to the people who gave him a position of great trust. The Secretary of State in attempting to justify his continued devotion to the man who sold out the Christian world to the atheistic world, referred to Christ's Sermon on the Mount as a justification and reason therefor, and the reaction of the American people to this would have made the heart of Abraham Lincoln happy.

When this pompous diplomat in striped pants, with a phony British accent, proclaimed to the American people that Christ on the Mount endorsed Communism, high treason, and betrayal of a sacred trust, the blasphemy was so great that it awakened the dormant indignation of the American people.

4

DOUGLAS MacARTHUR

Farewell Address to Congress

1951

Most Americans supported the cold war against communism, but they also feared nuclear war. Moderates would "contain" communism through conventional means that might avoid major war or the use of atomic weapons. Conservatives, fearing that containment might lead to accommodation and acceptance, wanted to "roll back" communism by various means, including, if necessary, the A-bomb. Korea crystallized these differences. General Douglas MacArthur, a World War II hero whose troops, under UN auspices, had successfully counterattacked North Korea only to encounter hordes of Chinese "volunteers," requested air strikes against China, which President Truman opposed. Frustrated, MacArthur publicly requested authorization to drop atomic bombs, urged an invasion of the mainland from Formosa, and dismissed containment as "appeasement." Truman fired him for insubordination.

The outcry was deafening. Newspapers called for the president's impeachment; crowds burned him in effigy. Meanwhile MacArthur traveled through adoring throngs to deliver a thirty-four-minute address to Congress (excerpted here) that was interrupted thirty times with cheers. One congressman called him the "voice of God"; others feared a coup d'état. In 1952 Republicans turned to Eisenhower, who ended the war and left Korea as divided as before. Moderates claimed victory, but conservatives still heard MacArthur's rhetoric ringing in their ears. On the Right, rage grew about the UN, Democratic cravenness, half-measures, and the dangers of military weakness. Most U.S. officers, traditionally nonpartisan but

Congressional Record (April 19, 1951).

chafing at containment's restraints, eventually became, like MacArthur,
conservative Republicans, a notable shift in military-rich states such as
California, Texas, and Florida.

I do not stand here as advocate for any partisan cause, for the issues
are fundamental and reach quite beyond the realm of partisan consideration. . . .

The Communist threat is a global one. Its successful advance in
one sector threatens the destruction of every other sector. You cannot
appease or otherwise surrender to Communism in Asia without simultaneously undermining our efforts to halt its advance in Europe. . . .

While I was not consulted prior to the President's decision to inter-
vene in support of the Republic of Korea, that decision, from a military
standpoint, proved a sound one, as we hurled back the invader and
decimated his forces. Our victory was complete and our objectives
within reach when Red China intervened with numerically superior
ground forces. This created a new war and an entirely new situation—
a situation not contemplated when our forces were committed against
the North Korean invaders—a situation which called for new decisions in the diplomatic sphere to permit the realistic adjustment of
military strategy. Such decisions have not been forthcoming.

While no man in his right mind would advocate sending our ground
forces into continental China and such was never given a thought, the
new situation did urgently demand a drastic revision of strategic planning if our political aim was to defeat this new enemy as we had
defeated the old.

Apart from the military need as I saw it to neutralize the sanctuary
protection given the enemy north of the Yalu, I felt that military necessity in the conduct of the war made mandatory:

1. The intensification of our economic blockade against China;
2. The imposition of a naval blockade against the China coast;
3. Removal of restrictions on air reconnaissance of China's coastal
   area and of Manchuria;
4. Removal of restrictions on the forces of the Republic of China
   on Formosa with logistic support to contribute to their effective operations against the common enemy.

For entertaining these views, all professionally designed to support
our forces committed to Korea and bring hostilities to an end with the
least possible delay and at a saving of countless American and Allied

lives, I have been severely criticized in lay circles, principally abroad, despite my understanding that from a military standpoint the above views have been fully shared in the past by practically every military leader concerned with the Korean campaign, including our own Joint Chiefs of Staff.

I called for reinforcements, but was informed that reinforcements were not available. I made clear that if not permitted to destroy the enemy buildup bases north of the Yalu; if not permitted to utilize the friendly Chinese force of some 600,000 men on Formosa; if not permitted to blockade the China coast to prevent the Chinese Reds from getting succor from without; and if there were to be no hope of major reinforcements, the position of the command from the military standpoint forbade victory. We could hold in Korea by constant maneuver and at an approximate area where our supply line advantages were in balance with the supply line disadvantages of the enemy, but we could hope at best for only an indecisive campaign, with its terrible and constant attrition upon our forces if the enemy utilized his full military potential. I have constantly called for the new political decisions essential to a solution. Efforts have been made to distort my position. It has been said that I was in effect a war monger. Nothing could be further from the truth. I know war as few other men now living know it, and nothing to me is more revolting. . . .

But once war is forced upon us, there is no other alternative than to apply every available means to bring it to a swift end. War's very object is victory—not prolonged indecision. In war, indeed, there can be no substitute for victory.

There are some who for varying reasons would appease Red China. They are blind to history's clear lesson. For history teaches with unmistakable emphasis that appeasement but begets new and bloodier war. It points to no single instance where the end has justified that means—where appeasement has led to more than a sham peace. Like blackmail, it lays the basis for new and successively greater demands, until, as in blackmail, violence becomes the only alternative. Why, my soldiers asked of me, surrender military advantages to an enemy in the field? I could not answer. Some may say to avoid spread of the conflict into an all-out war with China; others, to avoid Soviet intervention. Neither explanation seems valid. For China is already engaging with the maximum power it can commit and the Soviet will not necessarily mesh its actions with our moves. Like a cobra, any new enemy will more likely strike whenever it feels that the relativity in military or other potential is in its favor on a world-wide basis. . . .

I have just left your fighting sons in Korea. They have met all tests there and I can report to you without reservation they are splendid in every way. It was my constant effort to preserve them and end this savage conflict honorably and with the least loss of time and a minimum sacrifice of life. Its growing bloodshed has caused me the deepest anguish and anxiety. Those gallant men will remain often in my thoughts and in my prayers always.

I am closing my fifty-two years of military service. When I joined the Army even before the turn of the century, it was the fulfillment of all my boyish hopes and dreams. The world has turned over many times since I took the oath on the Plain at West Point, and the hopes and dreams have long since vanished. But I still remember the refrain of one of the most popular barrack ballads of that day which proclaimed most proudly that—

"Old soldiers never die, they just fade away."

And like the old soldier of that ballad, I now close my military career and just fade away—an old soldier who tried to do his duty as God gave him the light to see that duty.

5

RUSSELL KIRK

From *The Conservative Mind*

1953

Conservatism needed intellectual substance as well as political leaders, especially given the popularity of New Deal–Fair Deal programs. Russell Kirk helped provide that substance. While writing a dissertation in Scotland, which would become The Conservative Mind, *Kirk was profoundly influenced by the works of eighteenth-century British political*

Russell Kirk, *The Conservative Mind from Burke to Santayana* (Chicago: Henry Regnery Company, 1953), 7–10.

philosopher Edmund Burke. Its publication in 1953 was to be a key event in the history of U.S. conservatism.

Kirk provided conservatives with heroes from the American past, among them John Randolph, John Adams, and John C. Calhoun, all critics of mass movements, secularism, and the redistributive state. And he made devotion to the U.S. constitutional order, with its separation of powers, checks and balances, and divided sovereignty, a cornerstone of conservative ideology. Kirk's influence on conservative thinkers is difficult to overstate. After The Conservative Mind, *men such as William Rusher, future publisher of* National Review, *would become not "Republicans" but something they considered richer and deeper: "conservatives."*

There are six canons of conservative thought—

(1) Belief that a divine intent rules society as well as conscience, forging an eternal chain of right and duty which links great and obscure, living and dead. Political problems, at bottom, are religious and moral problems. A narrow rationality, what [poet Samuel Taylor] Coleridge calls the Understanding, cannot of itself satisfy human needs. "Every Tory is a realist," says Keith Feiling: "he knows that there are great forces in heaven and earth that man's philosophy cannot plumb or fathom. We do wrong to deny it, when we are told that we do not trust human reason: we do not and we may not. Human reason set up a cross on Calvary, human reason set up the cup of hemlock, human reason was canonised in Notre Dame." Politics is the art of apprehending and applying the Justice which is above nature.

(2) Affection for the proliferating variety and mystery of traditional life, as distinguished from the narrowing uniformity and equalitarianism and utilitarian aims of most radical systems. This is why Quintin Hogg (Lord Hailsham) and R. J. White describe conservatism as "enjoyment." It is this buoyant view of life which Walter Bagehot called "the proper source of an animated Conservatism."

(3) Conviction that civilized society requires orders and classes. The only true equality is moral equality; all other attempts at levelling lead to despair, if enforced by positive legislation. Society longs for leadership, and if a people destroy natural distinctions among men, presently Buonaparte fills the vacuum.

(4) Persuasion that property and freedom are inseparably connected, and that economic levelling is not economic progress. Separate property from private possession, and liberty is erased.

(5) Faith in prescription and distrust of "sophisters and calculators." Man must put a control upon his will and his appetite, for conservatives know man to be governed more by emotion than by reason. Tradition and sound prejudice provide checks upon man's anarchic impulse.

(6) Recognition that change and reform are not identical, and that innovation is a devouring conflagration more often than it is a torch of progress. Society must alter, for slow change is the means of its conservation, like the human body's perpetual renewal; but Providence is the proper instrument for change, and the test of a statesman is his cognizance of the real tendency of Providential social forces.

Various deviations from this system of ideas have occurred, and there are numerous appendages to it; but in general conservatives have adhered to these articles of belief with a consistency rare in political history. . . .

Radicalism since 1790 has tended to attack the prescriptive arrangement of society on the following grounds—

(1) The perfectibility of man and the illimitable progress of society: meliorism. Radicals believe that education, positive legislation, and alteration of environment can produce men like gods; they deny that humanity has a natural proclivity toward violence and sin.

(2) Contempt for tradition. Reason, impulse, and materialistic determinism are severally preferred as guides to social welfare, trustier than the wisdom of our ancestors. Formal religion is rejected and a variety of anti-Christian systems are offered as substitutes.

(3) Political levelling. Order and privilege are condemned; a total democracy, as direct as practicable, is the professed radical ideal. Allied with this spirit, generally, is a dislike of old parliamentary arrangements and an eagerness for centralization and consolidation.

(4) Economic levelling. The ancient rights of property, especially property in land, are suspect to almost all radicals; and collectivistic reformers hack at the institution of private property root and branch. . . .

The radical, when all is said, is a neoterist, in love with change; the conservative, a man who says with Joubert, *Ce sont les crampons qui unissent une génération à une autre* [These are the clamps that unite one generation with another]—these ancient institutions of politics and religion. . . .

If a conservative order is indeed to return, we ought to know the tradition which is attached to it, so that we may rebuild society; if it is not to be restored, still we ought to understand conservative ideas so that we may rake from the ashes what scorched fragments of civilization escape the conflagration of unchecked will and appetite.

6

WILLIAM F. BUCKLEY JR.

Publisher's Statement on Founding National Review

November 19, 1955

If Russell Kirk offered conservatives intellectual substance and a useable past, William F. Buckley offered them status, glamour, and combativeness. Buckley was from a large, wealthy, argumentative southern family that had relocated to Connecticut and took its right-wing politics and Roman Catholicism seriously. Buckley's God and Man at Yale *(1951) attacked his alma mater's hostility to religion and free enterprise and the academic freedom that sheltered such thinking. In 1954 he and his brother-in-law, L. Brent Bozell, published* McCarthy and His Enemies, *which endorsed McCarthy's methods and goals.*

Buckley's chief "movement" contribution came when he founded National Review, *an opinion weekly designed to do battle with* The Nation, The New Republic, *and other liberal publications, including* The New York Times *and other media too obtuse (or wicked) to see the danger of Soviet communism and the New Deal state. NR quickly became the nation's foremost right-wing periodical, not least because it reflected Buckley's taste for high-church religion, intellectual give and take, tony polysyllabic phrasing, and mordant witticisms. The first major movement figure from the eastern seaboard, Buckley's aristocratic aura was a far cry from the pedantic Taft, the folksy Thurmond, or the gruff McCarthy. With acolytes by the thousands, he became, in his biographer's phrase, a "patron saint" of the Right.*

The launching of a conservative weekly journal of opinion in a country widely assumed to be a bastion of conservatism at first glance looks like a work of supererogation, rather like publishing a royalist weekly within the walls of Buckingham Palace. It is not that, of course; if *National Review* is superfluous, it is so for very different reasons: It

William F. Buckley Jr., "Publisher's Statement on Founding *National Review*," *National Review*, November 19, 1955, 5.

stands athwart history, yelling Stop, at a time when no one is inclined to do so, or to have much patience with those who so urge it.

National Review is out of place, in the sense that the United Nations and the League of Women Voters and the *New York Times* and Henry Steele Commager are *in* place. It is out of place because, in its maturity, literate America rejected conservatism in favor of radical social experimentation. Instead of covetously consolidating its premises, the United States seems tormented by its tradition of fixed postulates having to do with the meaning of existence, with the relationship of the state to the individual, of the individual to his neighbor, so clearly enunciated in the enabling documents of our Republic.

"I happen to prefer champagne to ditchwater," said the benign old wrecker of the ordered society, Oliver Wendell Holmes, "but there is no reason to suppose that the cosmos does." We have come around to Mr. Holmes' view, so much so that we feel gentlemanly doubts when asserting the superiority of capitalism to socialism, of republicanism to centralism, of champagne to ditchwater—of anything to anything. (How curious that one of the doubts one is *not* permitted is whether, at the margin, Mr. Holmes was a useful citizen!) The inroads that relativism has made on the American soul are not so easily evident. One must recently have lived on or close to a college campus to have a vivid intimation of what has happened. It is there that we see how a number of energetic social innovators, plugging their grand designs, succeeded over the years in capturing the liberal intellectual imagination. And since ideas rule the world, the ideologues, having won over the intellectual class, simply walked in and started to run things.

Run just about *everything*. There never was an age of conformity quite like this one, or a camaraderie quite like the Liberals'. Drop a little itching powder in Jimmy Wechsler's bath and before he has scratched himself for the third time, Arthur Schlesinger will have denounced you in a dozen books and speeches, Archibald MacLeish will have written ten heroic cantos about our age of terror, *Harper's* will have published them, and everyone in sight will have been nominated for a Freedom Award. Conservatives in this country—at least those who have not made their peace with the New Deal, and there is serious question whether there are others—are nonlicensed nonconformists; and this is dangerous business in a Liberal world, as every editor of this magazine can readily show by pointing to his scars. Radical conservatives in this country have an interesting time of it, for when they are not being suppressed or mutilated by the Liberals, they are being ignored or humiliated by a great many of those of the well-fed Right, whose ignorance and amorality have never been exaggerated for the same reason that one cannot exaggerate infinity.

There are, thank Heaven, the exceptions. There are those of generous impulse and a sincere desire to encourage a responsible dissent from the Liberal orthodoxy. And there are those who recognize that when all is said and done, the market place depends for a license to operate freely on the men who issue licenses—on the politicians. They recognize, therefore, that efficient getting and spending is itself impossible except in an atmosphere that encourages efficient getting and spending. And back of all political institutions there are moral and philosophical concepts, implicit or defined. Our political economy and our high-energy industry run on large, general principles, on ideas—not by day-to-day guess work, expedients and improvisations. Ideas have to go into exchange to become or remain operative; and the medium of such exchange is the printed word. A vigorous and incorruptible journal of conservative opinion is—dare we say it?—as necessary to better living as Chemistry.

We begin publishing, then, with a considerable stock of experience with the irresponsible Right, and a despair of the intransigence of the Liberals, who run this country; and all this in a world dominated by the jubilant single-mindedness of the practicing Communist, with his inside track to History. All this would not appear to augur well for *National Review.* Yet we start with a considerable—and considered—optimism. . . .

Our own views, as expressed in a memorandum drafted a year ago, and directed to our investors, are set forth in an adjacent column. We have nothing to offer but the best that is in us. That, a thousand Liberals who read this sentiment will say with relief, is clearly not enough! It isn't enough. But it is at this point that we steal the march. For we offer, besides ourselves, a position that has not grown old under the weight of a gigantic, parasitic bureaucracy, a position untempered by the doctoral dissertations of a generation of Ph.D.'s in social architecture, unattenuated by a thousand vulgar promises to a thousand different pressure groups, uncorroded by a cynical contempt for human freedom. And that, ladies and gentlemen, leaves us just about the hottest thing in town.

7

NATIONAL REVIEW

Why the South Must Prevail

August 24, 1957

Buckley was primarily a warrior against communism and an apostle of free markets who understood that conservatives needed power if they were to roll back communism and the New Deal. Wresting the South from the Democrats would be a step toward such power. White southerners, however, were chiefly concerned with race, and although many Republicans, including some conservatives, disliked pandering to southern racism by endorsing states' rights, there seemed little alternative at the time.

This 1957 editorial on the composition of southern juries took a different tack: stressing regional racial traditions and capacities rather than constitutional principles. A reflection of Buckley's traditionalism, it also reflected a practical judgment: Political power mattered, and the way to power lay partly through the South. Never really supportive of the civil rights revolution, NR became even less so when Thurmond and others began to change parties. Buckley changed his position over the years, arguing in 1965 for disfranchising the unfit of all races and repudiating his 1957 stance in the 1970s, when overt racism had become an embarrassment. By then, however, the Republicans' conservative work in the South was well in hand.

In some parts of the South, the White community merely intends to prevail—that is all. It means to prevail on any issue on which there is corporate disagreement between Negro and White. The White community will take whatever measures are necessary to make certain that it has its way.

What are such issues? Is school integration one? The NAACP and others insist that the Negroes as a unit want integrated schools. Others disagree, contending that most Negroes approve the social separation of the races. What if the NAACP is correct, and the matter comes

"Why the South Must Prevail," editorial in *National Review*, August 24, 1957, 148–49.

to a vote in a community in which Negroes predominate? The Negroes would, according to democratic processes, win the election; but that is the kind of situation the White community will not permit. The White community will not count the marginal Negro vote. The man who didn't count it will be hauled up before a jury, he will plead not guilty, and the jury, upon deliberation, will find him not guilty. A federal judge, in a similar situation, might find the defendant guilty, a judgment which would affirm the law and conform with the relevant political abstractions, but whose consequences might be violent and anarchistic.

The central question that emerges—and it is not a parliamentary question or a question that is answered by merely consulting a catalogue of the rights of American citizens, born Equal—is whether the White community in the South is entitled to take such measures as are necessary to prevail, politically and culturally, in areas in which it does not predominate numerically? The sobering answer is *Yes*—the White community is so entitled because, for the time being, it is the advanced race. It is not easy, and it is unpleasant, to adduce statistics evidencing the median cultural superiority of White over Negro: but it is a fact that obtrudes, one that cannot be hidden by ever-so-busy egalitarians and anthropologists. The question, as far as the White community is concerned, is whether the claims of civilization supersede those of universal suffrage. The British believe they do, and acted accordingly, in Kenya, where the choice was dramatically one between civilization and barbarism, and elsewhere; the South, where the conflict is by no means dramatic, as in Kenya, nevertheless perceives important qualitative differences between its culture and the Negroes', and intends to assert its own.

National Review believes that the South's premises are correct. If the majority wills what is socially atavistic, then to thwart the majority may be, though undemocratic, enlightened. It is more important for any community, anywhere in the world, to affirm and live by civilized standards, than to bow to the demands of the numerical majority. Sometimes it becomes impossible to assert the will of a minority, in which case it must give way, and the society will regress; sometimes the numerical minority cannot prevail except by violence: then it must determine whether the prevalence of its will is worth the terrible price of violence.

The axiom on which many of the arguments supporting the original version of the Civil Rights bill were based was Universal Suffrage. Everyone in America is entitled to the vote, period. No right is prior to that, no obligation subordinate to it; from this premise all else proceeds.

That of course, is demagogy.... Millions who have the vote do not care to exercise it; millions who have it do not know how to exercise it and do not care to learn. The great majority of the Negroes of the South who do not vote do not care to vote, and would not know for what to vote if they could. Overwhelming numbers of White people in the South do not vote. Universal suffrage is not the beginning of wisdom or the beginning of freedom. Reasonable limitations upon the vote are not exclusively the recommendation of tyrants or oligarchists (was Jefferson either?). The problem in the South is not how to get the vote for the Negro, but how to equip the Negro—and a great many Whites—to cast an enlightened and responsible vote.

The South confronts one grave moral challenge. It must not exploit the fact of Negro backwardness to preserve the Negro as a servile class. It is tempting and convenient to block the progress of a minority whose services, as menials, are economically useful. Let the South never permit itself to do this. So long as it is merely asserting the right to impose superior mores for whatever period it takes to effect a genuine cultural equality between the races, and so long as it does so by humane and charitable means, the South is in step with civilization, as is the Congress that permits it to function.

8

ROBERT WELCH

From *The Blue Book of the John Birch Society*
1959

In 1958 Robert Welch, a Massachusetts candy maker and former director of the National Association of Manufacturers, created the John Birch Society, named for a Baptist missionary and army intelligence agent murdered by Communist Chinese in late 1945. With funding from con-

Robert Welch, *The Blue Book of the John Birch Society* (Boston and Los Angeles: Western Islands, 1957), 4–20, 33–46, 92, 117.

servative businesses, chapters in every state, the journal Public Opinion, *film strips showing Communist world control, and Welch's* The Blue Book *for required reading, the Birch Society became a leading grassroots conservative organization, with exceptional strength in the Sunbelt.*

In 1960 Welch circulated a manuscript entitled The Politician *that accused Eisenhower of being a "conscious communist agent." This partly discredited the Society, as did, for example, its obsession with water fluoridation as a subversive plot.* National Review *broke with Welch in the mid-1960s, arguing that the real domestic enemy was weak-kneed liberalism, not actual Communists.*

But the Society remained formidable. It influenced the Republican parties of Texas and California, helped Goldwater in 1964, and provided a base for Ronald Reagan. Its campaign to "Impeach Earl Warren" (integration was a Communist plot) anticipated later battles against liberal judges.* Its support for the anti–Equal Rights Amendment crusade anticipated the "family agenda" of the religious Right. NR targeted only Welch and not his members, who were the sort of shock troops the movement needed.

This material has been omitted intentionally in this reprint.

This material has been omitted intentionally in this reprint.

This material has been omitted intentionally in this reprint.

This material has been omitted intentionally in this reprint.

This material has been omitted intentionally in this reprint.

9

BARRY GOLDWATER

From *The Conscience of a Conservative*

1960

Most Americans considered "establishment" Republicans—Eisenhower, Nixon, Nelson Rockefeller—to be conservative: pro-business, pro–lower taxes, and anticommunist. The conservative movement saw them as temporizers ready to contain communism rather than roll it back, tolerate rather than terminate the New Deal, change race relations by federal edict, and accommodate labor unions. Believing that Nixon lost to John F. Kennedy in 1960 because he was too moderate, they found a "true" conservative to run in 1964.

In 1960 Barry Goldwater, a Sunbelt senator (R-AZ) who was unhappy with the centrist drift of his party, published a small book entitled The Conscience of a Conservative *that summarized the conservative position on labor unions and taxes, foreign and military policy, and federal versus states' rights. The plain-spoken book became an immediate best-seller, triggering a successful Draft Goldwater campaign that drew on Birch Society canvassers, endorsements from* National Review, *convention lobbying by Strom Thurmond, rallies by Young Americans for Freedom, and rousing campaign speeches by Ronald Reagan.*

This was an early flexing of conservative political muscle. Goldwater lost the election in part because he talked too freely about nuclear weapons. But he drew 27 million votes, a notable showing for so conservative a candidate. His supporters gained influence in party affairs.

Barry Goldwater, *The Conscience of a Conservative* (Washington, D.C.: Regnery Publishing, 1990), 18–19, 25–31, 52–60, 80, 83–85, 114–117.

*And by strenuously championing states' rights, he carried the Deep
South—a Republican first that would ultimately transform American
politics.*

Franklin Roosevelt's rapid conversion from Constitutionalism to the
doctrine of unlimited government is an oft-told story. But I am here
concerned not so much by the abandonment of States' Rights by the
national Democratic Party—an event that occurred some years ago
when that party was captured by the Socialist ideologues in and about
the labor movement—as by the unmistakable tendency of the Republican Party to adopt the same course. The result is that today *neither*
of our two parties maintains a meaningful commitment to the principle
of States' Rights. Thus, the cornerstone of the Republic, our chief bulwark against the encroachment of individual freedom by Big Government, is fast disappearing under the piling sands of absolutism. . . .

It is quite true that the integration issue is affected by the States'
Rights principle, and that the South's position on the issue is, today,
the most conspicuous expression of the principle. So much so that the
country is now in the grips of a spirited and sometimes ugly contro-
versy over an imagined conflict between States' Rights, on the one
hand, and what are called "civil rights" on the other. . . .

States' Rights are easy enough to define. The Tenth Amendment
does it succinctly: "The powers not delegated to the United States by
the Constitution nor prohibited by it to the States are reserved to the
States respectively, or to the people. . . .

A *civil* right is a right that is asserted and is therefore protected by
some valid law. It may be asserted by the common law, or by local or
federal statutes, or by the Constitution; *but unless a right is incorpo-
rated in the law, it is not a civil right and is not enforceable by the
instruments of the civil law.* . . .

The federal Constitution does *not* require the States to maintain
racially mixed schools. Despite the recent holding of the Supreme
Court, I am firmly convinced—not only that integrated schools are
not required—but that the Constitution does not permit any interference whatsoever by the federal government in the field of education.
It may be just or wise or expedient for negro children to attend the
same schools as white children, but they do not have a civil right to do
so which is protected by the federal constitution, or which is enforceable by the federal government.

The intentions of the founding fathers in this matter are beyond any doubt: *no powers regarding education were given the federal government.* Consequently, under the Tenth Amendment, jurisdiction over the entire field was reserved to the States. The remaining question is whether the Fourteenth Amendment—concretely, that amendment's "equal protection" clause—modified the original prohibition against federal intervention.

To my knowledge it has never been seriously argued—the argument certainly was not made by the Supreme Court—that the authors of the Fourteenth Amendment intended to alter the Constitutional scheme with regard to education. Indeed, in the famous school integration decision, *Brown v. Board of Education* (1954), the Supreme Court justices expressly acknowledged that they were not being guided by the intentions of the amendment's authors. *"In approaching this problem,"* Chief Justice Warren said, *"we cannot turn the clock back to 1868 when the amendment was adopted. . . . We must consider public education in the light of its full development and in its present place in American life throughout the nation."* In effect, the Court said that what matters is not the ideas of the men who wrote the Constitution, but the *Court's* ideas. It was only by engrafting its own views onto the established law of the land that the Court was able to reach the decision it did. . . .

It so happens that I am in agreement with the *objectives* of the Supreme Court as stated in the *Brown* decision. I believe that it *is* both wise and just for negro children to attend the same schools as whites, and that to deny them this opportunity carries with it strong implications of inferiority. I am not prepared, however, to impose that judgment of mine on the people of Mississippi or South Carolina, or to tell them what methods should be adopted and what pace should be kept in striving toward that goal. . . .

We have been led to look upon taxation as merely a problem of public financing: How much money does the government need? We have been led to discount, and often to forget altogether, the bearing of taxation on the problem of individual freedom. We have been persuaded that the government has an unlimited claim on the wealth of the people, and that the only pertinent question is what portion of its claim the government should exercise. The American taxpayer, I think, has lost confidence in *his* claim to his money. He has been handicapped in resisting high taxes by the feeling that he is, in the nature of things, obliged to accommodate whatever need for his wealth government chooses to assert. . . .

This attack on property rights is actually an attack on freedom. It is another instance of the modern failure to take into account the *whole* man. How can a man be truly free if he is denied the means to exercise freedom? How can he be free if the fruits of his labor are not his to dispose of, but are treated, instead, as part of a common pool of public wealth? Property and freedom are inseparable: to the extent government takes the one in the form of taxes, it intrudes on the other. . . .

The root evil is that the government is engaged in activities in which it has no legitimate business. As long as the federal government acknowledges responsibility in a given social or economic field, its spending in that field cannot be substantially reduced. As long as the federal government acknowledges responsibility for education, for example, the amount of federal aid is bound to increase, at the very least, in direct proportion to the cost of supporting the nation's schools. *The only way to curtail spending substantially, is to eliminate the programs on which excess spending is consumed.*

The government must begin to *withdraw* from a whole series of programs that are outside its constitutional mandate—from social welfare programs, education, public power, agriculture, public housing, urban renewal and all the other activities that can be better performed by lower levels of government or by private institutions or by individuals. . . .

And still the awful truth remains: We can establish the domestic conditions for maximizing freedom, along the lines I have indicated, and yet become slaves. We can do this by losing the Cold War to the Soviet Union. . . .

If an enemy power is bent on conquering you, and proposes to turn all of his resources to that end, he is at war with you; and you—unless you contemplate surrender—are at war with him. Moreover—unless you contemplate treason—your objective, like his, will be victory. Not "peace," but victory. Now, while traitors (and perhaps cowards) have at times occupied key positions in our government, it is clear that our national leadership over the past fourteen years has favored neither surrender nor treason. It is equally clear, however, that our leaders have not made *victory* the goal of American policy. And the reason that they have not done so, I am saying, is that they have never believed deeply that the Communists are in earnest.

Our avowed national objective is "peace." We have, with great sincerity, "waged" peace, while the Communists wage war. We have sought "settlements," while the Communists seek victories. We have tried to pacify the world. The Communists mean to own it. Here is why the contest has been an unequal one, and why, essentially, we are losing it. . . .

The rallying cry of an appeasement organization, portrayed in a recent novel on American politics,* was "I would rather crawl on my knees to Moscow than die under an Atom bomb." This sentiment, of course, repudiates everything that is courageous and honorable and dignified in the human being. We must—as the first step toward saving American freedom—affirm the contrary view and make it the cornerstone of our foreign policy: that we rather die than lose our freedom. . . . We want to stay alive, of course; but more than that we want to be free. We want to have peace; but before that we want to establish the conditions that will make peace tolerable. . . .

We must strive to achieve and maintain military superiority. Mere parity will not do. Since we can never match the Communists in manpower, our equipment and weapons must more than offset his advantage in numbers. We must also develop a limited war capacity. For this latter purpose, we should make every effort to achieve decisive superiority in small, clean nuclear weapons. . . .

The future, as I see it, will unfold along one of two paths. Either the Communists will retain the offensive; will lay down one challenge after another; will invite us in local crisis after local crisis to choose between all-out war and limited retreat; and will force us, ultimately, to surrender or accept war under the most disadvantageous circumstances. Or *we* will summon the will and the means for taking the initiative, and wage a war of attrition against them—and hope, thereby, to bring about the internal disintegration of the Communist empire. One course runs the risk of war, and leads, in any case, to probable defeat. The other runs the risk of war, and holds forth the promise of victory. For Americans who cherish their lives, but their freedom more, the choice cannot be difficult.

Advise and Consent by Allen Drury (published in 1959).

10

YOUNG AMERICANS FOR FREEDOM

The Sharon Statement

1960

Unlike the amorphous "New Left" of the 1960s, the conservative move-ment consisted mostly of adults with jobs, families, and sometimes politi-cal experience and ambitions. But the youth cohort was so enormous in midcentury America that it inevitably showed itself in conservative ranks—first among the Young Republican party affiliates and then in the Young Americans for Freedom.

YAF was founded in 1960 at a meeting of ninety young people at William F. Buckley's family estate in Sharon, Connecticut. Most of them were males from eastern "old-stock" middle-class families. Many were Catholic; some were Republican activists. The meeting established an or-ganizational structure and issued the Sharon Statement, which in later years took on, for conservatives, the same prophetic glow that Students for a Democratic Society's 1963 Port Huron Statement had for radicals.

There were tensions. Buckleyites chafed at opposition to mentioning God in the statement and fought the Birchers and Rockefeller supporters for control. Libertarians later criticized the military draft and antidrug laws. Even so, YAF became a much larger, more significant organization than SDS. YAF organized chapters across the country, published a newsletter, sponsored major national rallies, and worked for Goldwater and Reagan nationally. And until its demise in the 1980s, it served as a farm team for the right, producing, among others, Patrick Buchanan and Richard Viguerie.

In this time of moral and political crisis, it is the responsibility of the youth of America to affirm certain eternal truths.

We, as young conservatives, believe:

That foremost among the transcendent values is the individual's use of his God-given free will, whence derives his right to be free from the restrictions of arbitrary force;

www.yaf.com/index.shtml.

That liberty is indivisible, and that political freedom cannot long exist without economic freedom;

That the purposes of government are to protect these freedoms through the preservation of internal order, the provision of national defense, and the administration of justice;

That when government ventures beyond these rightful functions, it accumulates power which tends to diminish order and liberty;

That the Constitution of the United States is the best arrangement yet devised for empowering government to fulfill its proper role, while restraining it from concentration of power;

That genius of the Constitution—the division of powers—is summed up in the clause which reserves primacy to the several states, or to the people, in those spheres not specifically delegated to the Federal government;

That the market economy, allocating resources by the free play of supply and demand, is the single economic system compatible with the requirements of personal freedom and constitutional government, and that it is at the same time the most productive supplier of human needs;

That when government interferes with the work of the market economy, it tends to reduce the moral and physical strength of the nation; that when it takes from one man to bestow on another, it diminishes the incentive of the first, the integrity of the second, and the moral autonomy of both;

That we will be free only so long as the national sovereignty of the United States is secure; that history shows periods of freedom are rare, and can exist only when free citizens defend their rights against all enemies;

That the forces of international Communism are, at present, the greatest single threat to these liberties;

That the United States should stress victory over, rather than co-existence with, this menace; and

That American foreign policy must be judged by this criterion: does it serve the just interests of the United States?

11

MILTON FRIEDMAN

From *Capitalism and Freedom*

1962

Milton Friedman was a brilliant young intellectual who studied at the University of Chicago, the chief seat of free-market economic theory in the United States. He notably attended meetings of the Mt. Pelerin Society in Switzerland, the center of a so-called Austrian school of economists for whom state intervention was a "road to serfdom."

Friedman made three key arguments in the body of his work, which earned him a Nobel Prize in 1976. He believed that inflation, not unemployment, was the main modern economic problem and that inflation was a function purely of the money supply, which should be moderated through changes in interest rates rather than, as liberals believed, through the federal budget. He said that economic and political liberties go together and that to threaten one (through taxes and regulation) was to threaten the other. And he sharply criticized government programs. All of this was music to conservatives' ears, and Friedman became the Right's favorite economist.

We now have several decades of experience with governmental intervention. It is no longer necessary to compare the market as it actually operates and government intervention as it ideally might operate. We can compare the actual with the actual.

If we do so, it is clear that the difference between the actual operation of the market and its ideal operation—great though it undoubtedly is—is as nothing compared to the difference between the actual effects of government intervention and their intended effects. Who can now see any great hope for the advancement of men's freedom and dignity in the massive tyranny and despotism that hold sway in Russia? . . .

Let us look closer to home. Which if any of the great "reforms" of

---

Milton Friedman, *Capitalism and Freedom* (Chicago: University of Chicago Press, 1962), 197–200, 202.

past decades has achieved its objectives? Have the good intentions of the proponents of these reforms been realized? . . .

An income tax initially enacted at low rates and later seized upon as a means to redistribute income in favor of the lower classes has become a facade, covering loopholes and special provisions that render rates that are highly graduated on paper largely ineffective. . . . An income tax intended to reduce inequality and promote the diffusion of wealth has in practice fostered reinvestment of corporate earnings, thereby favoring the growth of large corporations, inhibiting the operation of the capital market, and discouraging the establishment of new enterprises. . . .

A housing program intended to improve the housing conditions of the poor, to reduce juvenile delinquency, and to contribute to the removal of urban slums, has worsened the housing conditions of the poor, contributed to juvenile delinquency, and spread urban blight.

In the 1930's, "labor" was synonymous with "labor union" to the intellectual community; faith in the purity and virtue of labor unions was on a par with faith in home and motherhood. Extensive legislation was enacted to favor labor unions and to foster "fair" labor relations. Labor unions waxed in strength. By the 1950's, "labor union" was almost a dirty word. . . .

Social security measures were enacted to make receipt of assistance a matter of right, to eliminate the need for direct relief and assistance. Millions now receive social security benefits. Yet the relief rolls grow and the sums spent on direct assistance mount.

The list can easily be lengthened: the silver purchase program of the 1930's, public power projects, foreign aid programs of the post-war years, F.C.C., urban redevelopment programs, the stockpiling program—these and many more have had effects very different and generally quite opposite from those intended. . . .

There can be little doubt that the record is dismal. The greater part of the new ventures undertaken by government in the past few decades have failed to achieve their objectives. The United States has continued to progress; its citizens have become better fed, better clothed, better housed, and better transported; class and social distinctions have narrowed; minority groups have become less disadvantaged; popular culture has advanced by leaps and bounds. All this has been the product of the initiative and drive of individuals co-operating through the free market. Government measures have hampered not helped this development. We have been able to afford and surmount these measures only because of the extraordinary fecundity of the market. . . .

The central defect of these measures is that they seek through government to force people to act against their own immediate interests in order to promote a supposedly general interest. They seek to resolve what is supposedly a conflict of interest, or a difference in view about interests, not by establishing a framework that will eliminate the conflict, or by persuading people to have different interests, but by forcing people to act against their own interest. They substitute the values of outsiders for the value of participants; either some telling others what is good for them, or the government taking from some to benefit others. . . .

The preservation and expansion of freedom are today threatened from two directions. The one threat is obvious and clear. It is the external threat coming from the evil men in the Kremlin who promise to bury us. The other threat is far more subtle. It is the internal threat coming from men of good intentions and good will who wish to reform us. Impatient with the slowness of persuasion and example to achieve the great social changes they envision, they are anxious to use the power of the state to achieve their ends and confident of their own ability to do so. Yet if they gained the power, they would fail to achieve their immediate aims and, in addition, would produce a collective state from which they would recoil in horror and of which they would be among the first victims. . . .

The two threats unfortunately reinforce one another. Even if we avoid a nuclear holocaust, the threat from the Kremlin requires us to devote a sizable fraction of our resources to our military defense. The importance of government as a buyer of so much of our output, and the sole buyer of the output of many firms and industries, already concentrates a dangerous amount of economic power in the hands of the political authorities, changes the environment in which business operates and the criteria relevant for business success, and in these and other ways endangers a free market. This danger we cannot avoid. But we needlessly intensify it by continuing the present widespread governmental intervention in areas unrelated to the military defense of the nation and by undertaking ever new government programs—from medical care for the aged to lunar exploration. . . .

I believe that we shall be able to preserve and extend freedom despite the size of the military programs and despite the economic powers already concentrated in Washington. But we shall be able to do so only if we awake to the threat that we face, only if we persuade our fellow men that free institutions offer a surer, if perhaps at times a slower, route to the ends they seek than the coercive power of the state.

12

RONALD REAGAN

Rendezvous with Destiny

October 24, 1964

Ronald Reagan, a California transplant from the Midwest, honed his communication and organizational skills as a radio announcer, movie actor, television personality, and officer in the actors' union. Initially a Democrat, he turned rightward in the 1950s while serving as the spokesman for General Electric, warning against big government, high taxes, and the Soviet menace. Already a favorite of Sunbelt conservatives, it was the following televised campaign speech for Barry Goldwater in October 1964 that gave him national stature and established him as one of the great voices and screen presences in American political history.

The speech not only helped Goldwater, it also helped shift the Republican center of gravity from the "establishment" East to the parvenu Sunbelt. As a result, conservatives rallied around Reagan's successful run two years later for governor of California, where he burnished his credentials by attacking progressive taxation, student and civil rights protestors, and government bureaucrats. He was to become the most popular governor in California history, and by 1976 he was ready for his own run for the Republican presidential nomination.

I have spent most of my life as a Democrat. I recently have seen fit to follow another course. I believe that the issues confronting us cross party lines. Now, one side in this campaign has been telling us that the issues of this election are the maintenance of peace and prosperity. The line has been used "We've never had it so good."

But I have an uncomfortable feeling that this prosperity isn't something on which we can base our hopes for the future. No nation in history has ever survived a tax burden that reached a third of its national income. Today, 37 cents of every dollar earned in this country is the tax collector's share, and yet our government continues to spend $17 million a day more than the government takes in. We haven't balanced our budget 28 out of the last 34 years. . . .

As for the peace that we would preserve, I wonder who among us would like to approach the wife or mother whose husband or son has died in South Vietnam and ask them if they think this is a peace that should be maintained indefinitely. Do they mean peace, or do they mean we just want to be left in peace? There can be no real peace while one American is dying some place in the world for the rest of us. We are at war with the most dangerous enemy that has ever faced mankind in his long climb from the swamp to the stars, and it has been said if we lose that war, and in doing so lose this way of freedom of ours, history will record with the greatest astonishment that those who had the most to lose did the least to prevent its happening. Well, I think it's time we ask ourselves if we still know the freedoms that were intended for us by the Founding Fathers.

Not too long ago two friends of mine were talking to a Cuban refugee, a businessman who had escaped from Castro, and in the midst of his story one of my friends turned to the other and said, "We don't know how lucky we are." And the Cuban stopped and said, "How lucky you are! I had someplace to escape to." In that sentence he told us the entire story. If we lose freedom here, there is no place to escape to. This is the last stand on Earth. And this idea that government is beholden to the people, that it has no other source of power except to sovereign people, is still the newest and most unique idea in all the long history of man's relation to man. This is the issue of this election. Whether we believe in our capacity for self-government or whether we abandon the American revolution and confess that a little intellectual elite in a far-distant capital can plan our lives for us better than we can plan them ourselves.

You and I are told increasingly that we have to choose between a left or right, but I would like to suggest that there is no such thing as a left or right. There is only an up or down—up to man's age-old dream, the ultimate in individual freedom consistent with law and order—or down to the ant heap totalitarianism, and regardless of their sincerity, their humanitarian motives, those who would trade our freedom for security have embarked on this downward course. . . .

We have so many people who can't see a fat man standing beside a thin one without coming to the conclusion that the fat man got that way by taking advantage of the thin one. So they are going to solve all the problems of human misery through government and government planning. Well, now, if government planning and welfare had the answer and they've had almost 30 years of it, shouldn't we expect government to almost read the score to us once in a while? Shouldn't they be telling us about the decline each year in the number of people needing help? The reduction in the need for public housing? . . .

So now we declare "war on poverty.". . . Now, do they honestly expect us to believe that if we add $1 billion to the $45 million we are spending . . . one more program to the 30-odd we have—and remember, this new program doesn't replace any, it just duplicates existing programs—do they believe that poverty is suddenly going to disappear by magic? Well, in all fairness I should explain that there is one part of the new program that isn't duplicated. This is the youth feature. We are now going to solve the dropout problem, juvenile delinquency, by reinstituting something like the old CCC camps, and we are going to put our young people in camps, but again we do some arithmetic, and we find that we are going to spend each year just on room and board for each young person that we help $4,700 a year! We can send them to Harvard for $2,700! Don't get me wrong. I'm not suggesting that Harvard is the answer to juvenile delinquency. . . .

I think we are for an international organization, where the nations of the world can seek peace. But I think we are against subordinating American interests to an organization that has become so structurally unsound that today you can muster a two-thirds vote on the floor of the General Assembly among the nations that represent less than 10 per cent of the world's population. I think we are against the hypocrisy of assailing our allies because here and there they cling to a colony, while we engage in a conspiracy of silence and never open our mouths about the millions of people enslaved in Soviet colonies in the satellite nation. . . .

Those who would trade our freedom for the soup kitchen of the welfare state have told us that they have a utopian solution of peace without victory. They call their policy "accommodation." And they say if we only avoid any direct confrontation with the enemy, he will forget his evil ways and learn to love us. All who oppose them are indicted as warmongers. They say we offer simple answers to complex problems. Well, perhaps there is a simple answer—not an easy answer—but simple.

If you and I have the courage to tell our elected officials that we want our national policy based upon what we know in our hearts is morally right, we cannot buy our security, our freedom from the threat of the bomb by committing an immorality so great as saying to a billion now in slavery behind the Iron Curtain, "Give up your dreams of freedom because to save our own skin, we are willing to make a deal with your slave masters." . . .

You and I know and do not believe that life is so dear and peace so sweet as to be purchased at the price of chains and slavery. If nothing in life is worth dying for, when did this begin—just in the face of this enemy? Or should Moses have told the children of Israel to live in slavery under the pharaohs? Should Christ have refused the cross? Should the patriots at Concord Bridge have thrown down their guns and refused to fire the shot heard 'round the world? The martyrs of history were not fools, and our honored dead who gave their lives to stop the advance of the Nazis didn't die in vain. Where, then, is the road to peace? Well, it's a simple answer after all.

You and I have the courage to say to our enemies, "There is a price we will not pay." There is a point beyond which they must not advance. This is the meaning in the phrase of Barry Goldwater's "peace through strength." . . .

You and I have a rendezvous with destiny. We will preserve for our children this, the last best hope of man on Earth, or we will sentence them to take the last step into a thousand years of darkness.

13

L. BRENT BOZELL

Who Is Accommodating to What?

May 4, 1965

Though not a major feature of midcentury conservatism, religion—especially Catholicism—was a major issue to some conservative thinkers, who saw it as a bulwark against Marxism and self-indulgent liberalism. Individual Catholics (Francis Cardinal Spellman, Joseph McCarthy) figured in the crusade against communism and subversion; National Review in particular possessed a high-church tone. But many American Christians were evangelical Protestants, historically fragmented and hos-

L. Brent Bozell, "Who Is Accommodating to What?" *National Review*, May 4, 1965, 374.

tile to Rome. American Catholics themselves, mostly of poor immigrant stock, supported New Deal–type programs that conservatives disliked. Catholics, moreover, seemed increasingly secular and individualistic, a trend made worse for conservatives by the Second Vatican Council (1962–1965), which permitted a host of innovations in worship, church participation, and political engagement.

This essay by L. Brent Bozell in National Review, *written just as Vatican II concluded, reflects traditionalist concerns over the state of the American church. William F.* Buckley's *Yale classmate and brother-in-law, Bozell was a stalwart who worked for Joe McCarthy, coauthored* McCarthy and His Enemies *with Buckley, and handled the Washington desk for* National Review *in the late 1950s. He was, however, increasingly critical of lax attitudes toward, for example, abortion and artificial birth control and of the hierarchy's refusal to call Catholics to account. Bozell eventually started a more conservative, openly Catholic journal and became, with his wife, a pioneer anti-abortion activist, providing inspiration for younger militants who would forge antiliberal alliances with Protestants as they worked to move Catholicism farther to the political right.*

I doubt whether one can exaggerate the trouble the Church is in. That is, of course, an *a priori* judgment: the mounting evidence of disarray, however dispiriting, could not in itself warrant historical pessimism in the light of the Church's demonstrated capacity for digging herself into and out of bigger messes than any that have brought empires down. What is different about the current disorders is that they are unattended by assurances that their perpetrators conceive Christianity as a *giver* of norms for judging the secular realm, rather than the other way around. What justifies alarm is the widespread willingness in the Church (eagerness is the word, of course, for the *avant garde*) to consult mirrors arranged by Christianity's enemies, so defined both by history and theology. . . .

In other ages, the heart of the Church, for all of its worldly distractions, was content with saving souls, an opportunity regarded as infinitely rich and expanding, notwithstanding that the means were understood to be static: the teaching of its own Truth, and providing conduits of Grace. Today the Church feels drawn to broader and more exciting horizons. Where these horizons lie, the innovators candidly profess not to know. But neither, it seems to me, have they paused to ponder whence the beckons come.

The striking thing about the innovations in Catholic thought is that they are innovations to no one but Catholics. The fresh air John XXIII is said to have let into the Church has understandably intoxicated the Catholic Left, by wafting away many of its frustrations; but for the rest of the world it is—all of it—very stale stuff. . . .

Consider the fresh ideas, still unanointed to be sure, that now blow freely out of the editorial offices of the Catholic press and down the corridors of the seminaries: population control and planned parenthood via contraceptive artifacts; mixed marriages with parents invited to slug it out over the children's souls, on an equal footing; proscription of capital punishment; a "dialogue" with homosexuals; nuns dressed like all the other ladies; priests as family men; religious liberty, meaning, concretely, an Open Door policy for Spain; racial equality as the age's transcendent moral command (opposition to racial discrimination, according to the editor of a diocesan weekly, "takes temporary priority over all other obligations including ecumenism and worship of God because of present conditions"); accommodation as the relevant mode of dealing with Communists; the preeminence of the social gospel (the Catholic twist: a holy war on poverty); the possibilities of constructing a theology on a study of fossils. These are the principal items of the current diet. . . .

Every one of them has its ancestry in the preoccupations of a world that has always viewed itself as laying siege at the walls of Rome. The point does not by itself disprove the thesis that *aggiornamento* [modernization] is divinely inspired; it does corroborate the intuition that it is Caesar, not the Holy Ghost, who has a corner on the attentions of a large part of the contemporary Church.

2

Expanding the Base, 1968–1980

14

George Wallace for President Brochure
1968

In 1962 Alabama Governor George Wallace, a Democrat, demanded "seg-regation forever," blocked the court-ordered admission of black students to the state university, and made himself a champion of the white South. After considering a run for the presidency in 1964, in 1968 he created the American Independent party and ran on that ticket. With funds generated by direct-mail guru Richard Viguerie and grassroots support from Birchers and segregationists, Wallace won five southern states (Richard Nixon took most of the rest) and captured blue-collar votes in the North.

Conservatives were of two minds about Wallace. His brand of "pop-ulist" conservatism posed a threat to the Republicans, whose victory margin was thin. Had Wallace taken more states (e.g., Florida, South Carolina—which Thurmond held for Nixon—and Texas—where LBJ prevailed) they might have lost. But Wallace's hard line on welfare, crime, and judicial coercion played well in the blue-collar North. Hubert Humphrey received only one-third of the white vote—the main reason for the 57 percent combined Wallace–Nixon total. This left an opening for Republicans who were more willing to adopt Wallace's posture.

A gunman shot and crippled Wallace in 1972 before he could com-plete another campaign. But as late as the mid-1970s Conservative Digest *readers considered Wallace one of their most important leaders. Republicans, said Wallace himself in 1981, took "a lot of their thoughts and their words and their principles from George Wallace."*

George Wallace for President 1968 Brochure, www.4president.org/brochures/wallace1968brochure.htm.

His views . . .

As Expressed in His Own Public Statements

ON LABOR

Issued executive order incorporating minimum union wage rates in all state contracts. Increased Workmen's and Unemployment Compensation benefits 37%. Promoted and passed legislation that reduced firemen's work week from 72 to 56 hours and substantially increased retirement pensions.

ON STATES' RIGHTS

I recommend that the states of the Union continue to determine the policies of their domestic institutions themselves and that the bureaucrats and theoreticians in Washington let people in Ohio and New York and California decide themselves . . . what type of school system they are going to have. I recommend states' rights and local government, and territorial democracy. . . .

ON CRIME

The first thing I would do as President is to make an announcement that I'd give my Moral Support as President to the policemen of this country and to the firemen of the country. I'd say, "We stand behind you because you are the thin line between complete anarchy in the streets and the physical safety of our person."

ON VIETNAM

. . . I think the first thing we ought to do in this country is to impress upon Hanoi and Peking and Moscow the resolve of the American people. These few people today who are out advocating sedition and raising money and clothes and supplies for the Viet Cong—these college professors who are making speeches advocating victory for the Viet Cong Communists—I would deal with these people as they ought to be dealt with, as traitors.

Constitutional Government

George C. Wallace is the undisputed leader in the fight for personal and property rights, and against excessive taxation and the takeover of personal rights by the "great society."

He believes in victory over Communism and Socialism at home and abroad.

15

SPIRO AGNEW

Two Speeches

October 20, 1969, and October 30, 1969

Nixon's running mate, Governor Spiro Agnew of Maryland, was a probusiness moderate who could bolster Republican chances in the West and the southern border states. Much criticized at the time for his lackluster record and low visibility, Vice President Agnew by 1969 had become indispensable in the administration's efforts to capitalize on the "backlash" against cultural and racial disorder, a role he came to relish.

Agnew leaned heavily on his speechwriters. The "Southern Strategy" was a province of Harry Dent, a former Thurmond aide. Pat Buchanan and others contributed language that attacked the mainstream media as "effete" and "snobbish" and unruly students as products of liberal permissiveness, echoing McCarthy and Wallace. Antipathy to demonstrations, strikes, and the often violent street politics abounded in Agnew's addresses.

The party faithful savored Agnew's attacks on snobs and social permissiveness and made him the Republicans' most popular speaker and most effective fund-raiser. By 1970 he was receiving 250 invitations a week; in fifteen appearances he raised $2.5 million. His contribution to Nixon's great 1972 victory was especially important given the defection of some conservatives over Nixon's overtures to China and Russia. Agnew resigned from the vice presidency in 1973 after being accused of taking bribes as governor and vice president in exchange for government favors.

October 20, 1969, Jackson, Mississippi

Very shortly the Supreme Court will consider a case involving desegregation of Mississippi schools. President Nixon is convinced that your public officials have made a strong case for additional time to implement the law without destroying quality education. The NAACP

John R. Coyne Jr., *The Impudent Snobs* (New York: Arlington House, 1972), 253–61.

disagrees and has brought this case to compel immediate action. It is hoped that the result will provide a sensible solution.

Much has been made of the Nixon administration's attitude toward the Southern states—mostly by the Northeastern liberal community. They've accused us of something, as you heard tonight, they call "The Southern Strategy." We have no Southern Strategy. We do have a conviction that the people of the United States, irrespective of their point of geographic residence, have an inherent right to be treated even-handedly by their government.

For too long the South has been the punching bag for those who characterize themselves as liberal intellectuals. Actually, they are consistently demonstrating the antithesis of intelligence. Their reactions are visceral, not intellectual; and they seem to believe that truth is revealed rather than systematically proved. These arrogant ones and their admirers in the Congress, who reach almost for equal arrogance at times, are bringing this nation to the most important decision it will ever have to make. They are asking us to repudiate principles that have made this country great. Their course is one of applause for our enemies and condemnation for our leaders. Their course is a course that will ultimately weaken and erode the very fibre of America. They have a masochistic compulsion to destroy their country's strength whether or not that strength is exercised constructively. And they rouse themselves into a continual emotional crescendo—substituting disruptive demonstration for reason and precipitate action for persuasion.

This group may consider itself liberal, but it is undeniable that it is more comfortable with radicals. These people use the word "compassion" as if they invented it. "Compassion" is their weapon and their shield. But they apply compassion selectively. Crime is excused only when the criminal is "disadvantaged."

They're equally selective as reformers. Waste in the Pentagon is a national outrage. Waste in welfare and poverty programs is a matter to be overlooked. . . .

This is the group that believes in marching down the streets of America to protest the war in Vietnam to our President. They would never think of protesting the continuation of this war to the government that is actually continuing it—the government of Hanoi. . . .

In my judgment, the principles of most of the people of Mississippi are the principles of the Republican Party. Since the policy makers of the other party have repudiated these principles, does it not make sense that Mississippi should become a strong state in the Republican column? It not only makes sense, but it's happening. The success of this gathering proves beyond question that it is happening.

October 30, 1969, Harrisburg, Pennsylvania

It is time for the preponderant majority, the responsible citizens of this country, to assert *their* rights. It is time to stop dignifying the immature actions of an arrogant, reckless, inexperienced element within our society. The reason is compelling. It is simply that their tantrums are insidiously destroying the fabric of American democracy.

By accepting unbridled protest as a way of life, we have tacitly suggested that the great issues of our times are best decided by posturing and shouting matches in the streets. America today is drifting toward Plato's classic definition of a degenerating democracy . . . a democracy that permits the voice of the mob to dominate the affairs of government.

Last week I was lambasted for my lack of "mental and moral sensitivity." I say that any leader who does not perceive where persistent street struggles are going to lead this nation lacks mental acuity. And any leader who does not caution this nation on the danger of this direction lacks moral strength. . . .

Ironically, it is neither the greedy nor the malicious, but the self-righteous who are guilty of history's worst atrocities. Society understands greed and malice and erects barriers of law to defend itself from these vices. But evil cloaked in emotional causes is well disguised and often undiscovered before it is too late.

We have just such a group of self-proclaimed saviours of the American soul at work today. Relentless in their criticism of intolerance in America, they themselves are intolerant of those who differ with their views. In the name of academic freedom, they destroy academic freedom. Denouncing violence, they seize and vandalize buildings of great universities. Fiercely expressing their respect for truth, they disavow the logic and discipline necessary to pursue truth.

They would have us believe that they alone know what is good for America; what is true and right and beautiful. They would have us believe that their reflective action is superior to our reflective action; that their revealed righteousness is more effective than our reason and experience.

Think about it. Small bands of students are allowed to shut down great universities. Small groups of dissidents are allowed to shout down political candidates. Small cadres of professional protesters are allowed to jeopardize the peace efforts of the President of the United States.

It is time to question the credentials of their leaders. And, if in questioning we disturb a few people, I say it is time for them to be disturbed. If, in challenging, we polarize the American people, I say it is time for a positive polarization.

It is time for a healthy in-depth examination of policies and a constructive realignment in this country. It is time to rip away the rhetoric and to divide on authentic lines. . . .

We have among us a glib, activist element who would tell us our values are lies, and I call them impudent. Because anyone who impugns a legacy of liberty and dignity that reaches back to Moses, is impudent.

I call them snobs for most of them disdain to mingle with the masses who work for a living. They mock the common man's pride in his work, his family and his country. It has also been said that I called them intellectuals. I did not. I said that they characterized themselves as intellectuals. No true intellectual, no truly knowledgeable person, would so despise democratic institutions.

America cannot afford to write off a whole generation for the decadent thinking of a few. America cannot afford to divide over their demagoguery . . . or to be deceived by their duplicity . . . or to let their license destroy liberty. We can, however, afford to separate them from our society—with no more regret than we should feel over discarding rotten apples from a barrel. . . .

Because on the eve of our nation's 200th birthday, we have reached the crossroads. Because at this moment totalitarianism's threat does not necessarily have a foreign accent. Because we have a home-grown menace, made and manufactured in the U.S.A. Because if we are lazy or foolish, this nation could forfeit its integrity, never to be free again.

16

FRANK S. MEYER

Defense of the Republic

April 7, 1970

America after 1965 seemed a sea of violence and destruction, with pervasive ghetto riots and antiwar demonstrations. Black violence helped feed George Wallace's national aspirations; student violence provoked Spiro Agnew's attacks on a spoiled generation. Law and order conservatives increasingly saw racial and student unrest as essentially similar efforts to overthrow the machinery of constitutional government.

A Princeton graduate and former Communist of eccentric habits and formidable intellect who helped organize YAF, the New York Conservative party, and the Goldwater for President movement, Frank Meyer was a mainstay of National Review *from 1957 until his death in 1972. Within the Buckleyite circle, Meyer was considered a "fusionist" who sought a political midpath between Kirk–Bozell traditionalism and the more libertarian versions of individualism. He supported federal and state regulation of rebellious behavior (mass riots and protest) that threatened constitutional order, opposed regulation of free-market capitalism, and urged unity on the Right around the anticommunist struggle.*

To preserve our republican social order, no radical extra-Constitutional steps are necessary. The Constitution and the laws on our statute books are generally sufficient, *if they are enforced.* At the most one or two additional interpretations, statutory or judicial, of the Constitution might be necessary. The sort of measures needed to re-establish order can be easily envisaged. Given the will to defend the Republic, they can be invoked; and, however startling they may seem in the present intellectual climate, they are certainly within the purview of the Constitution.

A few suggestions in this direction to indicate what can be done without a radical attack upon our established institutions:

Frank S. Meyer, "Defense of the Republic," *National Review*, April 7, 1970, 362.

Prosecution of all organizations (and their members) that stand for revolutionary attack upon our Constitutional institutions. Quick and decisive police action against all demonstrative assemblages attempting extra-legally to overawe political or private institutions, and the prosecution of participants under the relevant statutes for preservation of civil peace. (Our present state of civil peril may well make it necessary to ban all outdoor assemblages of a demonstrative nature, since they are avowedly directed toward overawing representative politics and thereby do not fit within the Constitutional right "peaceably to assemble and to petition the government for a redress of grievances.") The ending of social-worker and psychiatric attitudes toward crime; the full enforcement of criminal law; and reform of the probation system. All requisite increase and strengthening of our police forces, with, if necessary, the recruitment of an auxiliary part-time militia to augment their strength.

17

DONALD ATWELL ZOLL

Capital Punishment

December 3, 1971

Black riots and youth protests had decreased significantly by the early 1970s, but crime had not. Murder and aggravated assault rates doubled after the mid-1960s, forcible rape tripled, robbery quadrupled. Ordinary citizens felt besieged. When liberals failed to respond, conservatives called for more police, prisons, mandatory sentences, parole restrictions—and executions.

Capital punishment became one of the decade's hot issues, not least because liberals opposed it as "cruel and unusual" and the courts seemed prone to throw it out—which they did briefly in the mid-1970s. The death penalty therefore became a symbolic test of resolve to protect the public, a boon to hard-line Republicans. One of the clearest expositions of

Donald Atwell Zoll, "Capital Punishment," *National Review*, December 3, 1971, 1351–54.

the pro–death penalty position appeared in an essay for National Review
*by Donald Atwell Zoll, published just prior to the temporary court-man-
dated suspension of executions. Zoll had previously written for* NR *in
opposition to violent mass protests. His death penalty views extended this
preoccupation with public order.*

*There was a regional twist: The South had historically executed more
people than the North, and white Southerners were adamant for its
retention. When executions resumed in the late 1970s, eight of the ten
states with the highest number of executions (nearly a thousand, 80 percent of the total) were Southern. But support of capital punishment was
nationwide and led to, among other things, the creation of pro–death
penalty pressure groups and the recall of antiexecution judges in California and elsewhere.*

The supportive arguments on behalf of capital punishment finally
reduce, I think, to three:

1. *The Deterrent Argument.* . . .
2. *The Retaliation Argument.* . . .
3. *The Moral Indignation Argument.* . . .

While, on balance, the case for the retention of capital punishment
seems, to me, considerably more persuasive than its counterargu-
ments and, also, the prohibition of the death penalty by constitutional
injunction seems invalid, it appears very probable that the advocates
of abolition will have their way. I would not presume to try to plumb
the causes of their zeal for abolition that appears to fly in the face of
reason and experience. . . .

There is a very appreciable difference between a *humane* society
and an *effete* one. A humane society is a compassionate society, but
compassion is only significant in terms of justice, of a sensitivity to the
valid claims of men which rest upon the restraints on usurpation,
aggression and terror. The humane society does what is required to
preserve its incorporation of humanity. The effete society suffers from
a paralysis of will — and civilized enlightenment has never been characterized by a dormant or lethargic will.

A confused appreciation of the meaning of the "permissive society"
tempts many to exclude from it all vestiges of harshness, whatever
they may be, from abolishing the death penalty to discarding the use
of grades in schools. The death penalty or school grading systems

ought not to be retained merely because they are uncompromising, but because they serve desirable social ends, if, indeed, they do. The issue should turn on the social benefit and not on the superficial quality of the practice or the response it may elicit.

Capital punishment ought not to be abolished solely because it is substantially repulsive, if infinitely less repulsive than the acts which invoke it. Yet the mounting zeal for its abolition seems to arise from a sentimentalized hyperfastidiousness that seeks to expunge from the society all that appears harsh and suppressive. If we are to preserve the humane society we will have to retain sufficient strength of character and will to do the unpleasant in order that tranquility and civility may rule comprehensively. It seems very likely that capital punishment is a necessary, if limited factor in that maintenance of social tranquility and ought to be retained on this ground. To do otherwise is to indulge in the luxury of permitting a sense of false delicacy to reign over the necessity of social survival.

18

LEWIS F. POWELL JR.

Confidential Memorandum: Attack on American Free Enterprise System

August 23, 1971

Businessmen and conservatives worried about the antibusiness attitudes of the New Left and "counterculture" of the 1960s, particularly its anti-poverty and environmental rhetoric. Their efforts on behalf of Goldwater, Nixon, and, eventually, Reagan were one response. Some, however, including Lewis Powell, a leading corporation lawyer and former president of the American Bar Association whom Nixon would name to the Supreme Court, believed more was needed—that the battle required waging not just in politics but in public opinion, where university and media liberals seemed to be carrying the day.

"The Powell Memo," http://reclaimdemocracy.org/corporate_accountability/powell_memo_lewis.html.

Written for the U.S. Chamber of Commerce (and leaked to the press after Powell's Court confirmation), the memorandum prompted the Chamber to become a much more aggressive defender of capitalism and serves as an example of a broader phenomenon. In the 1970s money flowed from corporations, right-wing foundations, and wealthy families to institutions designed to do what Powell urged: defend free enterprise and shift the country's economic and political discussion to the right. Powell himself proved a centrist on the Court. He found that corporations could legally influence ballot questions but took moderate positions on affirmative action and abortion rights.

Dimensions of the Attack

No thoughtful person can question that the American economic system is under broad attack. This varies in scope, intensity, in the techniques employed, and in the level of visibility.

There always have been some who opposed the American system, and preferred socialism or some form of statism (communism or fascism). Also, there always have been critics of the system, whose criticism has been wholesome and constructive so long as the objective was to improve rather than to subvert or destroy.

But what now concerns us is quite new in the history of America. We are not dealing with sporadic or isolated attacks from a relatively few extremists or even from the minority socialist cadre. Rather, the assault on the enterprise system is broadly based and consistently pursued. It is gaining momentum and converts. . . .

The Apathy and Default of Business

What has been the response of business to this massive assault upon its fundamental economics, upon its philosophy, upon its right to continue to manage its own affairs, and indeed upon its integrity?

The painfully sad truth is that business, including the boards of directors and the top executives of corporations great and small and business organizations at all levels, often have responded—if at all—by appeasement, ineptitude and ignoring the problem. There are, of course, many exceptions to this sweeping generalization. But the net effect of such response as has been made is scarcely visible. . . .

A significant first step by individual corporations could well be the designation of an executive vice president (ranking with other executive

VP's) whose responsibility is to counter—on the broadest front—the attack on the enterprise system. The public relations department could be one of the foundations assigned to this executive, but his responsibilities should encompass some of the types of activities referred to subsequently in this memorandum. His budget and staff should be adequate to the task.

But independent and uncoordinated activity by individual corporations, as important as this is, will not be sufficient. Strength lies in organization, in careful long-range planning and implementation, in consistency of action over an indefinite period of years, in the scale of financing available only through joint effort, and in the political power available only through united action and national organizations.

Moreover, there is the quite understandable reluctance on the part of any one corporation to get too far out in front and to make itself too visible a target.

The role of the National Chamber of Commerce is therefore vital. Other national organizations (especially those of various industrial and commercial groups) should join in the effort, but no other organizations appear to be as well situated as the Chamber. It enjoys a strategic position, with a fine reputation and a broad base of support. Also—and this is of immeasurable merit—there are hundreds of local Chambers of Commerce which can play a vital supportive role. . . .

Staff of Scholars

The Chamber should consider establishing a staff of highly qualified scholars in the social sciences who do believe in the system. It should include several of national reputation whose authorship would be widely respected—even when disagreed with.

Staff of Speakers

There also should be a staff of speakers of the highest competency. These might include the scholars, and certainly those who speak for the Chamber would have to articulate the product of the scholars. . . .

Evaluation of Textbooks

The staff of scholars (or preferably a panel of independent scholars) should evaluate social science textbooks, especially in economics, political science and sociology. This should be a continuing program. . . .

Equal Time on the Campus

The Chamber should insist upon equal time on the college speaking circuit. The FBI publishes each year a list of speeches made on college campuses by avowed Communists. The number in 1970 exceeded 100. There were, of course, many hundreds of appearances by leftists and ultra liberals who urge the types of viewpoints indicated earlier in this memorandum. There was no corresponding representation of American business, or indeed by individuals or organizations who appeared in support of the American system of government and business. . . .

Television

The national television networks should be monitored in the same way that textbooks should be kept under constant surveillance. This applies not merely to so-called educational programs (such as "Selling of the Pentagon"), but to the daily "news analysis" which so often includes the most insidious type of criticism of the enterprise system. Whether this criticism results from hostility or economic ignorance, the result is the gradual erosion of confidence in "business" and free enterprise.

This monitoring, to be effective, would require constant examination of the texts of adequate samples of programs. Complaints—to the media and to the Federal Communications Commission—should be made promptly and strongly when programs are unfair or inaccurate.

Equal time should be demanded when appropriate. Effort should be made to see that the forum-type programs (the Today Show, Meet the Press, etc.) afford at least as much opportunity for supporters of the American system to participate as these programs do for those who attack it.

Other Media

Radio and the press are also important, and every available means should be employed to challenge and refute unfair attacks, as well as to present the affirmative case through these media.

The Scholarly Journals

It is especially important for the Chamber's "faculty of scholars" to publish. One of the keys to the success of the liberal and leftist faculty members has been their passion for "publication" and "lecturing." A similar passion must exist among the Chamber's scholars.

Incentives might be devised to induce more "publishing" by independent scholars who do believe in the system.

There should be a fairly steady flow of scholarly articles presented to a broad spectrum of magazines and periodicals—ranging from the popular magazines (*Life, Look, Reader's Digest,* etc.) to the more intellectual ones (*Atlantic, Harper's, Saturday Review, New York,* etc.) and to the various professional journals. . . .

Paid Advertisements

Business pays hundreds of millions of dollars to the media for advertisements. Most of this supports specific products; much of it supports institutional image making; and some fraction of it does support the system. But the latter has been more or less tangential, and rarely part of a sustained, major effort to inform and enlighten the American people.

If American business devoted only 10% of its total annual advertising budget to this overall purpose, it would be a statesman-like expenditure. . . .

Relationship to Freedom

The threat to the enterprise system is not merely a matter of economics. It also is a threat to individual freedom.

It is this great truth—now so submerged by the rhetoric of the New Left and of many liberals—that must be reaffirmed if this program is to be meaningful.

There seems to be little awareness that the only alternatives to free enterprise are varying degrees of bureaucratic regulation of individual freedom—ranging from that under moderate socialism to the iron heel of the leftist or rightist dictatorship. . . .

In addition to the ideological attack on the system itself (discussed in this memorandum), its essentials also are threatened by inequitable taxation, and—more recently—by an inflation which has seemed uncontrollable. But whatever the causes of diminishing economic freedom may be, the truth is that freedom as a concept is indivisible. As the experience of the socialist and totalitarian states demonstrates, the contraction and denial of economic freedom is followed inevitably by governmental restrictions on other cherished rights. It is this message, above all others, that must be carried home to the American people.

19

JEFF MacNELLY

"You in a Heap o' Trouble, Son"
March 17, 1972

*In the 1960s the Supreme Court fretted over the slowness of school deseg-
regation, a situation that reflected not only official stalling but residen-
tial patterns, "white flight" to the suburbs, and the popularity of private
schooling. In 1971 the Court permitted the busing of children away from
neighborhood schools, a decision that proved deeply unpopular not only
in the South but in the North, where schools were integral components of
neighborhoods bound by ethnicity, race, and class. This "forced busing"
was a catalyst for George Wallace's 1972 presidential run, during which
he showed strength in the South and the blue-collar North even after a
would-be assassin severely injured him. President Nixon, sensing the
issue's power, proclaimed his own opposition to additional busing schemes.*

No one poked sharper fun at busing than Jeff MacNelly of the News
Leader *newspaper in Richmond, Virginia, an epicenter of busing and
antibusing agitation. While MacNelly grew up admiring the work of liberal cartoonists such as Bill Mauldin and Herbert Block ("Herblock"),
who skewered the likes of Thurmond, Wallace, and Nixon, he worked for
conservative publications, was himself conservative—antitax, hostile to
Court orders on abortion and schools, tough on the cold war—and was
famous for his conservative comic strip,* Shoe. *As of his untimely death
in 2000, MacNelly had won three Pulitzer Prizes and blazed a trail for
conservative cartoonists.*

The Richmond News Leader, March 17, 1972.

'You in a heap o' trouble, son.'

20

RICHARD M. NIXON

Labor Day Radio Address

1972

Some conservatives such as Buckley, Welch, Wallace, and members of YAF intensely distrusted Richard Nixon. They felt he was too close to Eisenhower and Rockefeller, too soft on communism, uncommitted to states' rights, and willing to buy votes with government programs. Moreover, Nixon ran a cautious presidential campaign in 1960 and again in 1968. When Vice President Spiro Agnew resigned in 1973, Nixon teamed up with an equally suspicious centrist, Gerald Ford.

Richard M. Nixon, "Labor Day Radio Address," *The Clearest Choice* (n.p., 1972), 3–7.

However, a liberal climate and fear of nuclear war narrowed Nixon's options. Liberals certainly considered Nixon a conservative. He had hunted subversives, confronted Nikita Khrushchev in Moscow, favored big business, and advocated a strong military. Strom Thurmond supported him, as did Goldwater, most corporate executives, and, ultimately, Buckley. Milton Friedman was an adviser. This confidence seemed justified when Nixon nominated several conservatives for the Supreme Court (the Senate rejected two of them) and expanded the war in Indochina.

On the volatile race question, Nixon thought Goldwater's appeals to rabid segregationists were too crude to work outside the Deep South. He wanted instead to build (according to campaign memos) a "racial policy conservative enough to entice the South from Wallace" without losing northern blue-collar states. He did this partly by invoking a "silent majority" devoted to self-help and the work ethic, using racially coded language with broader appeal than "states' rights." In 1972, with Wallace crippled by a gunman, the strategy succeeded. Nixon proceeded, however, to corrupt the entire political system, thus triggering the Watergate scandal. Facing conviction on impeachment charges, he resigned the presidency in 1974, a year after Agnew.

The Worker's Values under Fire

On this Labor Day, I would like to discuss with you some of the decisions you will be facing this year—decisions that will affect your job, your paycheck, and your future.

Today, this Nation is operating under a system that is rooted in the values that built America:

—We believe that an able-bodied person should earn what he gets and keep most of what he earns. We must stop increases in taxes before they reach the point that the American wage earner is working more for the Government than he is for himself.

—We believe it is wrong for someone on welfare to receive more than someone who works.

—We believe that a person's ability and ambition should determine his income, and that his income should not be redistributed by Government or restricted by some quota system.

—We believe that when Government tampers too much with the lives of individuals, when it unnecessarily butts into the free collective bargaining process, it cripples the private enterprise system on which the welfare of the worker depends.

Because we have held fast to those values, the American worker has a higher standard of living and more freedom than any worker in the world today.

Work Ethic or Welfare Ethic?

We are faced this year with the choice between the "work ethic" that built this Nation's character and the new "welfare ethic" that could cause that American character to weaken.

Let's compare the two:

The work ethic tells us that there is really no such thing as "something for nothing," and that everything valuable in life requires some striving and some sacrifice. . . .

The welfare ethic, on the other hand, suggests that there is an easier way. It says that the good life can be made available to everyone right now, and that this can be done by the Government. . . .

The choice before the American worker is clear: The work ethic builds character and self-reliance, the welfare ethic destroys character and leads to a vicious cycle of dependency.

The work ethic builds strong people.

The welfare ethic breeds weak people. . . .

The Fallacy of Income Redistribution

Let me give you three specific examples of the difference between the work ethic and the welfare ethic, and how the choice directly affects your life.

The believers in the welfare ethic think it is unfair of some people to have much more income than others. They say we should begin right away to redistribute income, so that we can reduce the number of poor and bring about that day when everybody has much closer to the same income.

I believe that a policy of income redistribution would result in many more Americans becoming poor, because it ignores a human value essential to every worker's success—the incentive of reward.

It's human nature for a person who works hard for a living to want to keep most of what he earns, and to spend what he earns in the way he wants. Now, some may call this work ethic selfish or materialistic, but I think it is natural for a worker to resent seeing a large chunk of his hard-earned wage taken by Government to give to someone else who may even refuse to work. . . .

Quotas: Anti-ability, Anti-opportunity

A third traditional value that is coming under attack today by the welfare ethic has to do with ability, the great American idea that a person should be able to get ahead in life not on the basis of how he looks or who he knows, but rather on what he can do.

In employment and in politics, we are confronted with the rise of the fixed quota system—as artificial and unfair a yardstick as has ever been used to deny opportunity to anyone. . . .

Labor's Choice

Does the American workingman want to turn over a large part of his economic freedom, including much of his freedom to bargain collectively, to economic theorists who think they can permanently manage the economy?

Does the American workingman want to trade away opportunity for the false promise of government security?

Does the American workingman want his country to become militarily weak and morally soft?

I call upon working men and women across the Nation to make this Labor Day commitment: to understand all that is at stake for them and their families and to make their decision out of a conviction of what is best for themselves and best for all the people of America.

21

NATIONAL RIFLE ASSOCIATION

Act Before It Is Too Late

September 1974

Gun ownership was not a significant public issue until the 1970s, when Americans confronted a wave of assassinations, mass killings, riots, crime, graphic war reporting, and images of armed militants and National Guardsmen on university campuses. Since much of this violence involved firearms, one logical public response, especially among urban minorities and women, was to regulate firearm ownership. Another response, however, was to fight gun laws themselves as a threat to liberty and self-defense.

In 1974 the National Rifle Association established its Institute for Legislative Action, and articles in its magazine, The American Rifleman, *warned members of threats to their Second Amendment "right to keep and bear arms." NRA membership went up dramatically, as did support for the Second Amendment Foundation (1974) and similar organizations, each with its own publications and lobbyists. One of the first great "social" causes of the Right, the gun movement fit well with conservatism's overall demonization of the federal government. It also lured from the Democrats men for whom gun ownership was a "masculine tradition."*

It has been said—and truly—that there always seems to be a crisis over anti-gun laws.

That situation has haunted and harassed private gun ownership since the first gun controls were imposed in Europe in the 1500's and America in the 1600's.

Perhaps you think then, that things are no different today? They are different. They are getting worse. The gun control fight that has been going on at Federal and State levels off and on since the early 1900's is back at us—and there are more groups and misled news media in back of it than ever.

National Rifle Association, "Act Before It Is Too Late," *The American Rifleman*, September 1974, 22–23.

What stands between the law-abiding American gun owner and creeping confiscation of his guns? Little or nothing except The National Rifle Association of America and the grassroots will of a majority of the American public. That majority is largely unorganized and may be too big and loose to be organized.

So that leaves it to the NRA to express the will of its more than a million members, one of the most potent organized groups in the country, and also to marshal and speak for the multitude of individual gun owners who simply are not "joiners" or are not alert to the gravity of the impending crisis.

Fortunately for NRA Members and private gun ownership in the United States, the NRA is far better fitted and staffed today to combat anti-gun assaults than ever before in its 103-year history. It has, for the first time ever, a group of full-time expert lobbyists who are registered and authorized to speak in behalf of legitimate gun ownership in the Congress and in State Legislatures. For the first time ever, it has personnel detailed full-time to assist State and local groups of gun owners with their legislative problems. For the first time ever, it is using computerization to counter attacks on gun ownership.

Obviously, all of this costs money. Contrary to the untruths spread by anti-gun spokesmen, the NRA is not in any way financed or underwritten in such costs by the firearms manufacturers. Their advertising, while appreciated, does not even support *The American Rifleman*, much less the whole NRA.

So we have a problem—and it is a prime problem for all NRA Members and all others interested in legitimate firearms ownership to help solve. It boils down to one inevitable word: Money. To finance the massive legislative effort that is urgent to turn back new assaults on gun ownership, individual contributions to the new NRA Office of Legislative Affairs are gravely needed. This month, in this magazine, the NRA is formally soliciting your financial contributions to its legislative war chest. We are asking you because it is *your* campaign that we are waging.

Here are just some of the reasons why your assistance is urgently needed:

- No matter what happens over Watergate, it has stirred a tremendous political upheaval. Up to 100 or more of the 535 Senators and Congressmen in the next Congress will be newcomers, some of them anti-gun campaigners from heavily urban areas. Some longtime supporters of the right to bear arms, on the other hand, are retiring or facing desperate re-election fights. Someone must speak up for our side. That someone is your NRA legislative staff.

• In State elections, there is a similar likelihood of shakeups among lawmakers, though perhaps not as great. At any rate, someone must inform the new legislators on the facts about firearms and the uselessness of laws that attempt to control guns but fail to control criminals. That someone, again, is your NRA legislative staff.

• Also in the national arena there is a fresh movement out of Chicago to undermine legitimate gun ownership by outlawing ammunition rather than firearms. A new anti-gun lobby calling itself the Committee for Hand Gun Control, Inc., 111 E. Wacker Dr., Chicago, Ill., has petitioned the U.S. Consumer Product Safety Commission asking it to declare handgun cartridges "hazardous substances" and to prohibit them to all except military, police and security guards, and "licensed" pistol clubs. The commission, which admits it has no authority over firearms themselves, is to consider whether it can ban handgun ammunition. The Chicago group has dredged up misleading anti-gun propaganda to support its move.

• Already there is afoot in Washington, D.C., a new anti-gun organization preparing to work to influence the next Congress, it being virtually conceded that the present one is too busy to take up the gun control issue. The new organization is the Council to Control Handguns, 4114 Davis Pl., N.W., Washington, D.C.

• A number of State anti-gun groups are springing up, in Massachusetts, in Rhode Island with its Handgun Alert, Inc., and elsewhere. The NRA Office of Legislative Affairs has already created and tested a State program to counteract such anti-gun groups. The first such program has emerged as the Unified Sportsmen of Virginia, NRA-sponsored but open to all. It will serve as a model for similar programs elsewhere.

Members of the Office of Legislative Affairs (OLA) staff have already participated in turning back legislative attacks on gun ownership this spring in Massachusetts and Michigan. A coalition of three Michigan sportsmen's organizations—the NRA-affiliated Michigan Rifle and Pistol Association, the Michigan United Conservation Clubs, and the Sportsmen's Alliance of Michigan—defeated a petition drive to amend the Michigan constitution to outlaw handguns. The drive fell short by at least 60,000 signatures.

OLA is currently working on a computerization program which will improve the NRA's already efficient facilities for alerting the most involved groups of the million-plus membership to gun control issues.

22

NATHAN GLAZER

From *Affirmative Discrimination*

1975

Conservatives bitterly resented the extension of federal "affirmative action" mandates into higher education and the workplace. So did the "neoconservatives," a group of mostly Democratic writers and scholars who had provided intellectual firepower to the liberal cause since the 1930s. Although pro–New Deal, they were fiercely anticommunist. Many were Jews sensitive to racial categorizing and favoritism. They were also meritocratic; they resented intrusions, whether by radicals or federal mandates, into the institutions of higher learning that had educated and hired them because of their ability, not their group identity. Compensatory admissions and other group remedies were a particular breaking point for neocons, including sociologist Nathan Glazer, a member of the so-called New York Intellectuals—a group of anti-Stalinist, originally left-wing writers.

Other neocons included Daniel Patrick Moynihan, who worked for Nixon before winning a Democratic Senate seat from New York; Jeane Kirkpatrick, Reagan's UN ambassador; and Irving Kristol, who served on the editorial board of The Wall Street Journal. *Few in number, the neocons were prestigious and influential and provided intellectual heft for conservatism, which could now claim even liberalism's main publicists. As* National Review *put it in 1972: "Come on in, the water's fine."*

A new course in dealing with the issues of equality that arise in the American multiethnic society has been set since the early 1970s. It is demonstrated that there is discrimination or at least some condition of inequality through the comparison of statistical patterns, and then racial and ethnic quotas and statistical requirements for employment and school assignment are imposed. This course is not demanded

Nathan Glazer, *Affirmative Discrimination* (Cambridge, Mass., and London: Harvard University Press, 1975), 198–201.

by legislation—indeed, it is specifically forbidden by national legislation—or by any reasonable interpretation of the Constitution. Nor is it justified, I have argued, by any presumed failure of the policies of nondiscrimination and of affirmative action that prevailed until the early 1970s. Until then, affirmative action meant to seek out and prepare members of minority groups for better jobs and educational opportunities. (It still means only advertising and seeking out in the field of housing.) But in the early 1970s affirmative action came to mean much more than advertising opportunities actively, seeking out those who might not know of them, and preparing those who might not yet be qualified. It came to mean the setting of statistical requirements based on race, color, and national origin for employers and educational institutions. This new course threatens the abandonment of our concern for individual claims to consideration on the basis of justice and equity, now to be replaced with a concern for rights for publicly determined and delimited racial and ethnic groups.

The supporters of the new policy generally argue that it is a temporary one. They argue (or some do) that consideration of race, color, and national origin in determining employment and education is repugnant, but it is required for a brief time to overcome a heritage of discrimination. I have argued that the heritage of discrimination, as we could see from the occupational developments of the later 1960s, could be overcome by simply attacking discrimination. The statistical-pattern approach was instituted *after*, not before, the remarkably rapid improvement in the black economic and occupational position in the 1960s. I have argued that the claim that school assignment on the basis of race and ethnicity is only temporary is false, because the supporters of such an approach now demand it whatever the circumstances, and the Constitution is now so interpreted that it can be required permanently.

We have created two racial and ethnic classes in this country to replace the disgraceful pattern of the past in which some groups were subjected to an official and open discrimination. The two new classes are those groups that are entitled to statistical parity in certain key areas on the basis of race, color, and national origin, and those groups that are not. The consequences of such a development can be foreseen: They are already, in some measure, upon us. Those groups that are not considered eligible for special benefits become resentful. If one could draw a neat line between those who have suffered from discrimination and those who have not, the matter would be simpler. Most immigrant groups have had periods in which they were discriminated against. For the Irish and the Jews, for example, these periods lasted a long time. Nor is it the case that all the groups that are now recorded as deserving official protection have suffered discrimination, or in the same way. . . .

The protected groups include variously the descendants of free immigrants, conquered peoples, and slaves, and a single group may include the descendants of all three categories (e.g., the Puerto Ricans). Do free immigrants who have come to this country voluntarily deserve the same protected treatment as the descendants of conquered people and slaves? The point is that racial and ethnic groups make poor categories for the design of public policy. They include a range of individuals who have different legal bases for claims for redress and remedy of grievances. If the categories are designed to correct the injustices of the past, they do not work.

They do not work to correct the injustices of the present either, for some groups defined by race and ethnicity do not seem to need redress on the basis of their economic, occupational, and educational position. The Asian Americans have indeed been subjected to discrimination, legal and unofficial alike. But Chinese and Japanese Americans rank high in economic status, occupational status, educational status. (This does not prevent members of these groups from claiming the benefits that now accrue to them because they form a specially protected category under affirmative action programs.) If they were included in the protected category because they have faced discrimination, then groups in the unprotected categories also deserve inclusion. If they were included because they suffer from a poor economic, occupational, and educational position, they were included in error. So if these ethnic and racial categories have been designed to group individuals with some especially deprived current condition, they do not work well. Just as the Chinese and Japanese and Indians (from India) do not need the protection of the "Asian American" category, the Cubans do not need the protection of the Spanish-surnamed category, and middle-class blacks the protection of the Negro category, in order to get equal treatment today in education and employment. The inequalities created by the use of these categories became sharply evident in 1975 when many private colleges and universities tried to cut back on special aid for racially defined groups, who did indeed include many in need, but also included many in no greater need than "white" or "other" students. But the creation of a special benefit, whether needed or not, is not to be given up easily: Black students occupied school buildings and demanded that the privileges given on the basis of race be retained. This is part of the evil of the creation of especially benefited ethnic and racial categories. . . .

Compensation for the past is a dangerous principle. It can be extended indefinitely and make for endless trouble. Who is to determine what is proper compensation for the American Indian, the black, the Mexican American, the Chinese or Japanese American? When it is established that the full status of equality is extended to every individual, regardless of race, color, or national origin, and that special opportunity is also available to any individual on the basis of individual need, again regardless of race, color, or national origin, one has done all that justice and equity call for and that is consistent with a harmonious multigroup society.

23

ALAN CRAWFORD

The Taxfighters Are Coming!
November 1975

High taxes were anathema for Republicans, whose candidates invariably attacked Democrats as "tax-and-spenders." But the issue had little traction outside business circles, not least because moderates like Eisenhower and Nixon, though wanting lower taxes, feared the budget deficits that might follow. In the 1970s, however, property values, demand for state services, energy costs, interest rates, and unemployment all escalated together. The resultant rising taxes and falling disposable income provoked citizen anger. This early "tax revolt" reached critical mass in 1978 in California, where former Goldwaterite Howard Jarvis orchestrated a ballot initiative pegging local taxes to 1 percent of property values. Voters passed it overwhelmingly, and eventually other states passed similar measures.

"No New Taxes" also surged nationally, with the federal income tax its main target. The Chamber of Commerce and other business organizations joined the fray, as did the Birch Society, the Liberty Lobby, and the

Alan Crawford, "The Taxfighters Are Coming!" *Conservative Digest*, November 1975, 13–14.

racist Aryan Nations, some of whose adherents resorted to armed tax resistance. Mostly, the movement consisted of suburbanites tired of paying the bills for bureaucrats and minorities and seeking some relief. They were a bedrock, as tax reduction was a mantra, of the Republican majorities to come.

Alan Crawford, a former YAF activist, was an editor for Conservative Digest, *founded by Richard Viguerie in 1975 to build a sense of momentum and provide a forum for conservative voices. He broke with Viguerie and the Right a few years later, charging them with distortion and deception.*

More than 900 residents of Willimantic, Conn., crowded into a town meeting last January to voice their opposition to high taxes assessed by the city government. After a tumultuous debate, the citizens triumphed, slashing a proposed city budget by a whopping nine percent.

The meeting climaxed a 45-day taxpayers' revolt in which the city of 15,000 refused to authorize their city officials to spend, tax or borrow even one cent. Under Willimantic's 1893 charter, major decisions are made by direct vote of virtually all adult residents.

"We certainly got the message," Willimantic's 30-year-old mayor, David J. Calchera, said.

"The depth of their anger was incredible," commented Richard Jackson, a leader of the revolt.

$200,000 was trimmed from a proposed $2.6 million budget—a savings of almost $50 to the average Willimantic home owner. Eliminated were such marginal items as five school crossing guards, a clerk and a new car for the fire department.

The Willimantic Revolt was not an isolated incident but part of a growing national trend. Aroused by soaring taxes, spiraling inflation, increased unemployment and rising public debt, angry taxpayers are telling the public officials they elected, "Cut taxes and spending!"

SCRANTON, PA.—"Taxes are already too high," Leo Lynn of the Taxpayer's Association of Lackawanna County, Pa., told *Conservative Digest.* "We've got 15 percent unemployment here. Our city (Scranton) is already six million dollars in debt and the interest on our bonded indebtedness is $1,100 a day. The budgets are too high and now they are trying to pass a bill so they can buy a new street cleaner."

According to spokesman Lynn, Scranton residents first organized in the late '60s, when they were angered over taxes that took greater and greater chunks out of their paychecks. They formed the Homeowners and Taxpayer's League, which lobbied against the first U.S.-Soviet grain deal, contending it was inflationary.

The group has since become the Taxpayer's Association of Lackawanna County (TALC).

"Our main purpose," Lynn explained, "is to lower taxes—which in this state is almost impossible."

Pennsylvania law has no provision for a referendum or recall to allow voters to express their disapproval of proposed budgets. "Once our leaders are elected," Lynn explained, "we can't do a thing about their spending. This leaves us no legal recourse, short of withholding our taxes.

"What we're really fighting," he said, "is taxation without representation, taxation without legislation." . . .

MAINE—Citizens of the peaceful coastal communities along eastern Maine are awaiting a court verdict on their tax revolt.

Upset by what they consider unfair property assessments, more than ten communities have joined together to fight a new education tax law.

Albert Barnes, state editor of the *Portland Press-Herald* explained, "These towns traditionally have worked out their own contracts with public schools, funding the schools themselves. And generally they seemed happy with the situation."

But, Barnes said, a new state law was passed requiring owners to pay higher school taxes as property values go up. In recent years, property values along the Maine coast have increased so citizens there are paying higher taxes to support the state school system.

This conflicts with contracts the coastal communities have already entered into with local school districts.

The protesting communities include Harpswell, Boothbay, Boothbay Harbor, Castine, Bowdoinham, Mt. Desert, Cranberry Isle, Friendship, Cushing, Topsham and Georgetown. . . .

ARIZONA—Tax fighters here have formed the Arizona Caucus Club, all of whose members are active tax resisters and meet periodically in Mesa, Ariz.

In Maricopa County, L. Marvin Cooley, author of "Tea Party 1976," and W. Vaughn Ellsworth, author of "The 5th Amendment Tax Packet," both handbooks for tax resisters, are leading similar groups of tax fighters. Their handbooks contain information regarding the filing of income tax reports and how to use the 5th Amendment in answering questions. . . .

"There are now over five million tax resisters in the U.S.," Baxter estimated. "That's 10 percent of the 50 million taxpayers employed in private industry."

"In case there is any confusion," Baxter told *Conservative Digest,* "we are not advocating that people break the law. In fact, the law is on our side. Not necessarily the courts, but the law and the constitution.

"All the American people have to do is to obey the law, tell the truth, stand up for their rights and maintain their status as law-abiding citizens.

"When they claim that they have no income—since, after all, the Federal Reserve Bank closed its accounts in 1968—the IRS backs off because this approach attacks the very tax system. It attacks the IRS, the Federal Reserve System and the U.S. Treasury."

24

PHYLLIS SCHLAFLY

Interview with the Washington Star

January 18, 1976

In 1972 both houses of Congress overwhelmingly passed an Equal Rights Amendment that prohibited discrimination on the basis of gender. Within a year, the legislatures of thirty of the thirty-eight states needed for ratification had endorsed the amendment. With bipartisan support, including Nixon's, adoption looked certain.

It was, however, not to be—thanks to the efforts of Phyllis Schlafly. Schlafly was an Illinois lawyer with a record of Republican activism and militant anticommunism. In 1973, alarmed at the ERA's progress and the possibility of federal interference with the traditional family, she organized STOP ERA. A devout Catholic, she enlisted the help of fellow Catholic Richard Viguerie to raise funds, got mailing lists from conservative societies, and contacted hundreds of concerned Mormons, Baptists, Methodists, and members of the Churches of Christ, most of them women, to influence legislators, especially in the Midwest, South, and West.

"Interview with Phyllis Schlafly," *Washington Star,* January 18, 1976.

By 1975 STOP ERA (later Eagle Forum) had 50,000 members. Their efforts halted the ratification movement at thirty-five states, three short of the two-thirds needed. This was one of the earliest multidenominational church-based conservative crusades, suggesting its great potential for the future. The involvement of Mormons, heretofore standoffish, was particularly significant. Utah's senators, Jake Garn and Orrin Hatch, would become conservative heroes in the Reagan era. Schlafly meanwhile served notice that the National Organization for Women and other feminist groups were not the sole voices speaking on behalf of American women, a victory for Republicans among women.

Question: What do you make of the recent setbacks of the Equal Rights Amendment and the defeat of the state equal rights amendments in New York and New Jersey?

Schlafly: I think they show that despite the fact that the proponents had nearly 100 percent of the press on their side, and despite the fact that they had nearly 100 percent of the politicians who cared to commit themselves on their side, nevertheless the voters recognized ERA as a fraud, and they're against it. They recognize it as a takeaway of women's rights; they recognize it won't do anything good for women, and so they're against it.

Q: Why do you feel that if women got legal equality, say in New York, it would take away their rights?

Schlafly: The New York state support law is a beautiful law. It says the husband must support his wife, and the husband must support their minor children under age 21. It's perfectly obvious that when you apply the ERA to that law, it becomes immediately unconstitutional.

So ERA will take away the right of the wife to be supported and to have her minor children supported. Obviously, this is an attack on the rights of the wife and on the family. The principal thing that ERA does is to take away the right of the wife in an ongoing marriage, the wife in the home.

Q: Do you think that that is the reason men support their wives, because it's the law?

Schlafly: Yes, I do. Because it is their duty, and I think duty is an honorable word. When men get married they know that they are taking on the duty of supporting their wives.

Q: Do you think that women today really are getting married to be supported?

Schlafly: Even if you think that in the future the law should be changed, I think it is a gross invasion of the property rights of women in existing marriages to come along and say, "Now as a new principle of law—no matter that you went into marriage 10, 20, 30, 40 years ago, thinking that the marriage contract meant a definite relationship—too bad, sister. You're on your own now." And that's what they're saying.

Q: You see it happening that the wife at some point would have to support the husband?

Schlafly: She would be equally liable for the financial support.

Q: What's wrong with that?

Schlafly: What's wrong with that? Because you can't make the having of babies equally shared. I think our laws are entitled to reflect the natural differences and the role assigned by God, in that women have babies and men don't have babies.

Therefore, the wife has the right to support, and the husband has the duty to pay for the groceries on the table. Anything that ERA does to that is a takeaway of what she has now. It's a reduction in those rights. And even if you want to discuss alimony or child support or divorced women, in any state where alimony is something that goes only from husband to wife, which is half the states, ERA knocks it out, because it isn't equal.

Q: You mean the women might have to pay alimony.

Schlafly: Sure, that's right. And the proponents say this is what they want.

Q: Well, do you really see anything wrong with a woman paying alimony if she has the money and her husband doesn't?

Schlafly: The thing that's so fraudulent about ERA is that it is presented as something which will benefit women, which will lift women out of this second-class citizenship, this oppression that they've allegedly been in for the last 200 years. The proponents cannot show any single way that ERA is going to benefit women.

Q: You are also against the women's movement?

Schlafly: I certainly am.

Q: Why is that?

Schlafly: I think it is destructive and antifamily. I think their goals can be summed up as, first, for ERA, which is a takeaway of the legal rights that wives now have. Second, it is pro-abortion on demand, and government-financed abortion and abortion in government hospitals or any hospitals. Third, it's for state nurseries, to get the children in the nurseries and off the backs of the mothers.

Fourth, it is for prolesbian legislation, which is certainly an anti-marriage movement. And fifth, it is for changing the school textbooks in order to eliminate what they call the stereotype of woman in the home as wife and mother. So I consider that all five of their principle objectives are antifamily.

Q: Do you think that women would be as well off today were it not for the women's movement?

Schlafly: I certainly do. There were more women in Congress prior to the women's movement than there are today.

Q: Well, haven't there been a lot of other gains, though? There are many more women working today and a lot of them are getting better salaries too.

Schlafly: And a lot of them who are working would prefer to be in the home. They are working for economic reasons.

Q: But if they have to work then it's important that they make as much money as they can, at least as much as men, for what they are doing.

Schlafly: I believe in equal pay for equal work. I do not believe in hiring unqualified women over qualified men to remedy some alleged oppression of 25 years ago.

Q: Do you think that people are being forced to hire this way?

Schlafly: Yes, we had a good example of that recently in a federal court, a ruling that has ordered the Chicago Police Department to hire 16 percent women, on a quota. Now in order to do this they have got to throw out the physical qualifications that are required to be a policeman on the Chicago police force. And I feel this is absolutely wrong.

It's hurtful to men, it's hurtful to women and it's hurtful to the community. And it will do nothing but demoralize and destroy the police force.

Q: You think the women will not be able to perform the job as well as men?

Schlafly: That's correct. The same thing's true in the military. There is an honorable place for women in the military. They have the best of both worlds in the military today. They are protected from combat service and from some of the dangerous and unpleasant jobs in the military.

I feel that ERA, which would require identical treatment in combat, and in the draft the next time we have one of these wars, is hurtful to everybody. It's hurtful to the defense of our country, it's terribly hurtful to our young women, it's hurtful to the women who want to make a career in the military and it's hurtful to the men.

Q: Don't you think that the women who want to be in the service should be the ones to make that decision?

Schlafly: You mean the decision as to whether they go into combat? No, I certainly don't. I think the purpose of the military is to defend our country in battle. The purpose is not to provide on-the-job training for somebody who thinks she wants a fun career with a lot of men around.

Q: You feel that women need to be protected in many ways?

Schlafly: I feel that there are physical differences between men and women. The women's lib movement establishes as dogma that there is no difference between men and women except the sex organs. I think this is nonsense.

25

COMMITTEE ON THE PRESENT DANGER

Common Sense and the Common Danger

1976

By the mid-seventies, the Vietnam debacle had left the public skeptical of military intervention and the military itself in problematic condition. The Soviets were expanding their nuclear forces and meddling in Central America and the Middle East while Jimmy Carter, ex-Navy and a southern businessman but still a Democrat, was talking about human rights and internationalism and Pentagon restructuring. Troubled cold warriors of every stripe responded with the Committee on the Present Danger (CPD), a nonpartisan (though predominantly Republican) group dedicated to sounding the alarm about the Soviets and rebuilding American resolve and strength.

Charles Tyroler III, ed., *Alerting America* (Washington, D.C.: Pergamon-Brassey's Publishers, 1984), 3–5.

Though led by cold warriors from the Johnson and Nixon years, the CPD immediately attracted strong support from younger right-wingers, including the neoconservatives, who were publicizing Soviet human rights and blamed the Kremlin for dictator Anastazio Somoza's overthrow in Nicaragua and the struggle to control the Panama Canal. The CPD lobbied successfully against ratification of the SALT II treaty, which limited nuclear weapons, and accused Carter of weakness after the fall of the Shah of Iran and the Soviet invasion of Afghanistan in the late 1970s. For the CPD, these mistakes resulted from weak political resolve, inadequate military power, and an underestimation of global challenges.

I

Our country is in a period of danger, and the danger is increasing. Unless decisive steps are taken to alert the nation, and to change the course of its policy, our economic and military capacity will become inadequate to assure peace with security.

The threats we face are more subtle and indirect than was once the case. As a result, awareness of danger has diminished in the United States, in the democratic countries with which we are naturally and necessarily allied, and in the developing world.

There is still time for effective action to ensure the security and prosperity of the nation in peace, through peaceful deterrence and concerted alliance diplomacy. A conscious effort of political will is needed to restore the strength and coherence of our foreign policy; to revive the solidarity of our alliances; to build constructive relations of cooperation with other nations whose interests parallel our own—and on that sound basis to seek reliable conditions of peace with the Soviet Union, rather than an illusory detente. . . .

II

The principal threat to our nation, to world peace, and to the cause of human freedom is the Soviet drive for dominance based upon an unparalleled military buildup. . . .

For more than a decade, the Soviet Union has been enlarging and improving both its strategic and its conventional military forces far more rapidly than the United States and its allies. Soviet military power and its rate of growth cannot be explained or justified by considerations of self-defense. The Soviet Union is consciously seeking what its spokesmen call "visible preponderance" for the Soviet sphere. Such preponderance, they explain, will permit the Soviet Union "to transform the conditions of world politics" and determine the direction of its development.

The process of Soviet expansion and the worldwide deployment of its military power threaten our interest in the political independence of our friends and allies, their and our fair access to raw materials, the freedom of the seas, and in avoiding a preponderance of adversary power.

These interests can be threatened not only by direct attack, but also by envelopment and in direct aggression. The defense of the Middle East, for example, is vital to the defense of Western Europe and Japan. In the Middle East the Soviet Union opposes those just settlements between Israel and its Arab neighbors which are critical to the future of the area. Similarly, we and much of the rest of the world are threatened by renewed coercion through a second round of Soviet-encouraged oil embargoes.

III

Soviet expansionism threatens to destroy the world balance of forces on which the survival of freedom depends. If we see the world as it is, and restore our will, our strength and our self-confidence, we shall find resources and friends enough to counter that threat. There is a crucial moral difference between the two superpowers in their character and objectives. The United States—imperfect as it is—is essential to the hopes of those countries which desire to develop their societies in their own ways, free of coercion.

To sustain an effective foreign policy, economic strength, military strength, and a commitment to leadership are essential. We must restore an allied defense posture capable of deterrence at each significant level and in those theaters vital to our interests. The goal of our strategic forces should be to prevent the use of, or the credible threat to use, strategic weapons in world politics; that of our conventional forces, to prevent other forms of aggression directed against our interests. Without a stable balance of forces in the world and policies of collective defense based upon it, no other objective of our foreign policy is attainable.

As a percentage of Gross National Product, U.S. defense spending is lower than at any time in twenty-five years. For the United States to be free, secure and influential, higher levels of spending are now required for our ready land, sea, and air forces, our strategic deterrent, and, above all, the continuing modernization of those forces through research and development. The increased level of spending required is well within our means so long as we insist on all feasible efficiency in our defense spending. We must also expect our allies to bear their fair share of the burden of defense.

From a strong foundation, we can pursue a positive and confident diplomacy, addressed to the full array of our economic, political and social interests in world politics. It is only on this basis that we can expect successfully to negotiate hardheaded and verifiable agreements to control and reduce armaments.

If we continue to drift, we shall become second best to the Soviet Union in overall military strength; our alliances will weaken; our promising rapprochement with China could be reversed. Then we could find ourselves isolated in a hostile world, facing the unremitting pressures of Soviet policy backed by an overwhelming preponderance of power. Our national survival itself would be in peril, and we should face, one after another, bitter choices between war and acquiescence under pressure.

26

EUGENE H. METHVIN

The NEA: A Washington Lobby Run Rampant
November 1978

Although social issues — crime, busing, guns, women's rights, affirmative action — expanded the conservative agenda of the 1970s, economics remained important, as in the tax revolt, militant defense of capitalism, and the resurgence of the National Right to Work Committee, an anti-union organization that gained several hundred thousand members and became a formidable lobby. A media epicenter of anti-unionism was Reader's Digest, *which had the highest circulation of any American*

Eugene H. Methvin, "The NEA: A Washington Lobby Run Rampant," *Reader's Digest,* November 1978, 97–101.

magazine and was conservative in its views: anticommunism, low taxes, free markets, self-help, religion, and the dangers of organized labor.

Eugene Methvin used the forum of Reader's Digest *to attack the National Education Association, a union of schoolteachers that grew dramatically in the 1970s. NEA made an ideal target for conservatives. It was a public-sector union committed to higher teacher salaries and more programs, hence more spending and higher taxes, and more federal involvement, hence less community control. It also supported liberal "social engineering" (busing and affirmative action) rather than the trusty "three r's" of traditional education.*

Georgia-born Methvin wrote many Digest *pieces on unions, including their ties to organized crime. A conservative authority on crime, Methvin argued that police, not antipoverty programs, would stop crime and riots. An author of two books on the topic and a contributor to* National Review *and other right-wing journals, he also served on President Reagan's Commission on Organized Crime. The Methvin family sponsored an annual Confederate Memorial Day that flew the Stars and Bars just miles "from the Yankee White House."*

This material has been omitted intentionally in this reprint.

This material has been omitted intentionally in this reprint.

This material has been omitted intentionally in this reprint.

27

HUGH HAYNIE

American Weakness

September 1979

Conservatives stridently opposed the renewed negotiations to limit nuclear arms ("SALT II"), arguing that the agreement would favor the USSR and tie American hands in resisting Soviet incursions in the Caribbean, especially Cuba, where the Soviets reportedly had combat troops. Hugh Haynie's cartoon for the Louisville Courier-Journal *reflects these animosities: Soviet firepower, welcomed by Cuba's bearded leader Fidel Castro, prepares to blow the foolish dove of arms control to smithereens. The Haynie cartoon was typical of the Right's assault on President Jimmy Carter's foreign policy. As a side benefit, the constant portrayal of Castro as a security threat helped win the loyalties of Florida's Cuban exile community, which conservatives hoped would join disaffected whites, military personnel, gun owners, and evangelical Protestants in a permanent Republican majority in that crucial state.*

Louisville Courier-Journal, September 1979.

"... Ready on the left ...!"

28

PAUL WEYRICH

Building the Moral Majority
August 1979

Religion played a relatively minor role on the Right until the 1970s, when religious conservatives turned from anticommunism and resistance to segregation to face new challenges to their faith and families in the form of women's rights, secular education, legalized abortion, and homosexuality. They grew alarmed in 1978 when the Carter administration threatened to end the tax exemption of the hundreds of Christian schools

Paul Weyrich, "Building the Moral Majority," *Conservative Digest*, August 1979, 18–19.

that white southerners had established after desegregation. Church militants forced a reversal and then girded for battle.

In 1979 Paul Weyrich, Richard Viguerie, and others met with Jerry Falwell, a minister of a large Southern Baptist church in Virginia who had his own television program, about building a "moral majority" that would unite Protestants and Catholics against "secular humanists" by stressing their common "family values" and opposition to abortion, gays, and feminism. Within a year the Moral Majority (an echo of Nixon's "silent majority") claimed 400,000 members. Falwell was briefly the most influential preacher in the country, eagerly dispensing his version of Republican gospel: low taxes, military strength, anticommunism — and family values.

Weyrich, a Wisconsin Catholic, former Republican senatorial aide, and founder of the Heritage Foundation, was the main architect of the Moral Majority. Weyrich saw the Moral Majority as an agent in a "culture war" of Christians against abortionists and other liberals that, like the law and order, progun, and antiwelfare movements, could enhance the Republican party's appeal among ordinary voters, especially in the South and Midwest.

The family will be to the decade of the 1980s what environmentalism and consumerism have been to the 1970s and what the Vietnam war was to the 1960s.

It is possible that the enemies of the family and society may at last have set up a situation where the majority in this nation who still subscribe to moral principles and traditional values can unite into a cohesive political movement to change the direction of the country.

There was, in fact, a moral majority of sorts who were in power in this country for many years, into the early part of this century. But the Scopes trial and the revolt against Prohibition swept these fundamentalists, if you will, out of power, and they have been on the defensive ever since, until recent times.

Television and the new breed of religious leader, exemplified by the Rev. Jerry Falwell and by Pat Robertson of the 700 Club, have given life and effectiveness to the Word of God as articulated by these men, who are not ashamed to pronounce that the Bible is the unerring truth. Unlike many of their predecessors, these "electronic preachers" understand the linkage between the religious and moral issues and the politics of our time.

Meanwhile, the Second Vatican Council of the Catholic Church has produced a whole new dimension which its modernist advocates did not intend. The liberal Catholic promoters of the excesses of Vatican II had a vision of a one-world Church, void of doctrine and beliefs, united at last with the "near beer" versions of mainline Protestantism. It is true, of course, that since Vatican II the social gospel advocates in the Catholic and Protestant churches have been working ever more closely together. But the "ecumaniacs" had not counted on a reverse coalition. Now, however, the true-believing Gospel-oriented Catholics, having been told by the hierarchy that they should seek accommodation with their Protestant brethren, have taken to working with fundamentalist/evangelical Protestants in, for example, the right-to-life movement rather than with liberal Protestants in boycotting grapes with Cesar Chavez.

The alliance has produced great results. The media often portray the right-to-life movement as a tool of the Catholic bishops. Movement insiders know it is a truly grassroots effort and that if anything the Catholic bishops have hindered its success. Any typical right-to-life gathering these days is a microcosm of the moral majority, with urban ethnic Catholics, Gospel-believing Protestants, Mormons and Orthodox Jews working together.

The upshot of this new alliance is that hundreds of thousands, perhaps millions, of lives have been saved because of the visibility of the issue. We never hear about these lives. They don't make the statistical counts. These are the babies born of the mothers who have heard the message that abortion is murder.

Because of the strong political reaction against abortion, the necrophiliac agenda for euthanasia, limiting the number of children a family may have (population control) and other overt antifamily schemes has been slowed down considerably.

And the movement has given teenagers of this generation a cause, something more important than themselves, for which to work. In this "era of the self," no other political movement has managed to accomplish anything like it.

What the right-to-life movement has managed to put together on the abortion issue is only a sample of what is to come when the full range of family and educational issues becomes the focus of debate in the 1980s.

The homosexual rights advocates, genetic engineers and militant secular humanists who insist on their religion in the schools had better understand what is happening.

The threat to the family has caused leaders of various denominations to put aside their sectarian differences and, for the first time in decades, agree on basic principles worth fighting for. This is no false unity based on papering over doctrinal differences. The various leaders of the individual communities have given up none of their beliefs in order to cooperate. Rather, the pro-family movement is a recognition that the moral majority must be put together as a coalition — because our very right to worship as we choose, to bring up our families in some kind of moral order, to educate our children free from the interference of the state, to follow the commands of Holy Scripture and the Church are at stake. These leaders have concluded it is better to argue about denominational differences at another time. Right now, it is the agenda of those opposed to the Scriptures and the Church which has bought us together. . . .

The alliance of which Falwell spoke has great potential and political implications. Clear-cut moral choices can be offered the American voter for the first time in decades. The alliance on family issues is bound to begin to look at the morality of other issues such as SALT and the unjust power that has been legislated for union bosses.

What is more, all of this occurs at a time when the political parties have declined to the point where, in certain parts of the country, they are no longer taken seriously.

It is a coalition which can work. It can be the basis for a Christian democratic movement rooted in the authentic Gospel, not the social gospel.

Each part of the coalition brings something useful. The fundamentalist/evangelical Protestants bring a knowledge of and devotion to the Bible which no politician can shake. In addition, they have mastered the use of television and radio for their efforts, and this will make communications easier. The Catholics and Eastern Orthodox bring philosophical underpinnings which can help make the coalition impervious to attack, so that this alliance will not be swept away as happened earlier in this century. The Catholics also bring with them their rich cultural traditions from places like Ireland and Italy which can serve well during these times of attack on the family. The Mormons bring a superb knowledge of organization and outreach, and the Orthodox Jews bring not only family tradition but the ability to be productively aggressive.

29

RONALD REAGAN

Nomination Acceptance Speech

1980

By the fall of 1980 the Republicans were a profoundly conservative party with a strong influence in the South, in the churches, and among gun owners, cold warriors, family traditionalists, antiwelfare suburbanites, corporate tax cutters, and economic deregulators. Fate gave them an opponent—Jimmy Carter—whose standing was undercut by gasoline shortages, a severe economic slump, and helplessness in the face of the hostage crisis in Iran. It also supplied a centrist third-party candidate—John Anderson—who hurt Democrats even more than Republicans.

They also boasted Ronald Reagan, their longtime hero, around whom all factions could rally. Reagan's carefully cultivated "common man" image—plaid work shirt, disarming grin, warm voice, relaxed body posture, sense of humor, confident manner—fit with Republican efforts to seem like "just folks" rather than corporate executives. Reagan began his campaign by touting states' rights à la Thurmond, Goldwater, and Wallace at the site of an infamous civil rights murder in Mississippi. But he had broad appeal and carried forty-four states in the election—including the entire South except for Georgia, Carter's home state.

As president, Reagan acted decisively, a contrast with the cautious Carter. He fired striking air traffic controllers and destroyed their union; permitted development, including oil drilling, in wilderness and wetlands; ordered the invasion of Grenada; got Congress to cut income and capital gains taxes; and dramatically increased defense spending. He termed the resulting deficits "supply-side economics," a novel policy that, he said, would increase investment, employment, and, eventually, tax collections.

Never before in our history have Americans been called upon to face three grave threats to our very existence, any one of which could destroy us. We face a disintegrating economy, a weakened defense, and an energy policy based on the sharing of scarcity. . . .

I will not stand by and watch this great country destroy itself under mediocre leadership that drifts from one crisis to the next, eroding our national will and purpose. We have come together here because the American people deserve better from those to whom they entrust our nation's highest offices, and we stand united in our resolve to do something about it. . . .

First, we must overcome something the present administration has cooked up: new and altogether indigestible economic stew, one part inflation, one part high unemployment, one part recession, one part runaway taxes, one part deficit spending and seasoned by an energy crisis. It's an economic stew that has turned the national stomach.

Ours are not problems of abstract economic theory. Those are problems of flesh and blood; problems that cause pain and destroy the moral fiber of real people who should not suffer the further indignity of being told by the government that it is all somehow their fault. We do not have inflation because—as Mr. Carter says—we have lived too well.

The head of a government which has utterly refused to live within its means and which has, in the last few days, told us that this year's deficit will be $60 billion, dares to point the finger of blame at business and labor, both of which have been engaged in a losing struggle just trying to stay even.

High taxes, we are told, are somehow good for us, as if, when government spends our money it isn't inflationary, but when we spend it, it is.

Those who preside over the worst energy shortage in our history tell us to use less, so that we will run out of oil, gasoline, and natural gas a little more slowly. Conservation is desirable, of course, for we must not waste energy. But conservation is not the sole answer to our energy needs.

America must get to work producing more energy. The Republican program for solving economic problems is based on growth and productivity.

Large amounts of oil and natural gas lay beneath our land and off our shores untouched because the present administration seems to believe the American people would rather see more regulation, taxes and controls than more energy.

Coal offers great potential. So does nuclear energy produced under rigorous safety standards. It could supply electricity for thousands of industries and millions of jobs and homes. It must not be thwarted by a tiny minority opposed to economic growth which often finds friendly ears in regulatory agencies for its obstructionist campaigns. . . .

Our federal government is overgrown and overweight. Indeed, it is time for our government to go on a diet. Therefore, my first act as chief executive will be to impose an immediate and thorough freeze on federal hiring. Then, we are going to enlist the very best minds from business, labor and whatever quarter to conduct a detailed review of every department, bureau and agency that lives by federal appropriations. We are also going to enlist the help and ideas of many dedicated and hard working government employees at all levels who want a more efficient government as much as the rest of us do. I know that many are demoralized by the confusion and waste they confront in their work as a result of failed and failing policies.

Our instructions to the groups we enlist will be simple and direct. We will remind them that government programs exist at the sufferance of the American taxpayer and are paid for with money earned by working men and women. Any program that represents a waste of their money—a theft from their pocketbooks—must have that waste eliminated or the program must go—by executive order where possible; by congressional action where necessary. Everything that can be run more effectively by state and local government we shall turn over to state and local government, along with the funding source to pay for it. We are going to put an end to the money merry-go-round where our money becomes Washington's money, to be spent by the states and cities exactly the way the federal bureaucrats tell them to. . . .

I have long advocated a 30 percent reduction in income tax rates over a period of three years. This phased tax reduction would begin with a 10 percent "down payment" tax cut in 1981, which the Republicans [in] Congress and I have already proposed.

A phased reduction of tax rates would go a long way toward easing the heavy burden on the American people. But, we should not stop here.

Within the context of economic conditions and appropriate budget priorities during each fiscal year of my presidency, I would strive to go further. This would include improvement in business depreciation taxes so we can stimulate investment in order to get plants and equipment replaced, put more Americans back to work and put our nation back on the road to being competitive in world commerce. We will also work to reduce the cost of government as a percentage of our gross national product. . . .

When we move from domestic affairs and cast our eyes abroad, we see an equally sorry chapter on the record of the present administration.

— A Soviet combat brigade trains in Cuba, just 90 miles from our shores.

— A Soviet army of invasion occupies Afghanistan, further threatening our vital interests in the Middle East.

— America's defense strength is at its lowest ebb in a generation, while the Soviet Union is vastly outspending us in both strategic and conventional arms.

— Our European allies, looking nervously at the growing menace from the East turn to us for leadership and fail to find it.

— And, incredibly more than 50 of our fellow Americans have been held captive for over eight months by a dictatorial foreign power [Iran] that holds us up to ridicule before the world. . . .

Can we doubt that only a Divine Providence placed this land, this island of freedom, here as a refuge for all those people in the world who yearn to breathe freely: Jews and Christians enduring persecution behind the Iron Curtain, the boat people of Southeast Asia, of Cuba and Haiti, the victims of drought and famine in Africa, the freedom fighters of Afghanistan and our own countrymen held in savage captivity.

I'll confess that I've been a little afraid to suggest what I'm going to suggest—I'm more afraid not to—that we begin our crusade joined together in a moment of silent prayer. God bless America.

3

Clean Sweep, 1980–2000

30

GEORGE GILDER

From *Wealth and Poverty*

1981

George Gilder's 1981 best seller Wealth and Poverty *took the argument for untrammeled capitalism to extremes not seen for more than a century. Pure free enterprise, argued Gilder, not welfare or redistribution, was the path to prosperity for the poor as well as the nation. There might be more inequality, but there would also be more capitalists — hence investment, hence economic growth, hence jobs for people who were willing to work, a willingness that welfare necessarily undermined.*

Gilder was also a harsh critic of feminism — "America's number-one antifeminist," in his own words — for thwarting male ambition and family responsibility, major sources of the work ethic. Gilder's free-market evangelism and seeming answers to the problem of poverty — work, marry, have faith — were a huge hit with conservatives, mostly because they implied lower taxes, and helped shape Republican attitudes to problem solving for the next thirty years.

It is only individuals who can be original. Institutions shy away from unproven or unfashionable ideas. Therefore, they cannot afford to create new knowledge. It is the rich who by risking their wealth ultimately lose it, and save the economy. . . .

George Gilder, *Wealth and Poverty* (New York: Basic Books, 1981), 63, 68–70, 72–73, 127, 268.

The risk-bearing role of the rich cannot be performed so well by anyone else. The benefits of capitalism still depend on capitalists. The other groups on the pyramid of wealth should occasionally turn from the spectacles of consumption long enough to see the adventure on the frontiers of the economy above them—an adventure not without its note of nobility, since its protagonist families will almost all eventually fail and fall in the redeeming struggle of the free economy.

... Under capitalism, when it is working, the rich have the anti–Midas touch, transforming timorous liquidity and unused savings into factories and office towers, farms and laboratories, orchestras and museums—turning gold into goods and jobs and art. That is the function of the rich: fostering opportunities for the classes below them in the continuing drama of the creation of wealth and progress. . . .

The only dependable route from poverty is always work, family, and faith. The first principle is that in order to move up, the poor must not only work, they must work harder than the classes above them. Every previous generation of the lower class has made such efforts. But the current poor, white even more than black, are refusing to work hard. . . .

The current poor work substantially less, for fewer hours and weeks a year, and earn less in proportion to their age, education, and other credentials (even *after* correcting the figures for unemployment, disability, and presumed discrimination) than either their predecessors in American cities or those now above them on the income scale. . . . Current welfare and other subsidy programs substantially reduce work. The poor choose leisure not because of moral weakness, but because they are paid to do so.

A program to lift by transfers and preferences the incomes of less diligent groups is politically divisive—and very unlikely—because it incurs the bitter resistance of the real working class. In addition, such an effort breaks the psychological link between effort and reward, which is crucial to long-run upward mobility. Workers have to understand and feel deeply that what they are given depends on what they give—that they must supply work in order to demand goods. . . .

After work the second principle of upward mobility is the maintenance of monogamous marriage and family. Adjusting for discrimination against women and for child-care responsibilities, [a] Wisconsin study indicates that married men work between two and one-third and four times harder than married women, and more than twice as hard as female family heads. The work effort of married men increases with their age, credentials, education, job experience, and birth of children, while the work effort of married women steadily declines. Most important in judging the impact of marriage, husbands work 50 percent harder than bachelors of comparable age, education, and skills.

The effect of marriage, thus, is to increase the work effort of men by about half. Since men have higher earnings capacity to begin with, and since the female capacity-utilization figures would be even lower without an adjustment for discrimination, it is manifest that the maintenance of families is the key factor in reducing poverty.

Once a family is headed by a woman, it is almost impossible for it to greatly raise its income even if the woman is highly educated and trained and she hires day-care or domestic help. . . .

The short-sighted outlook of poverty stems largely from the breakdown of family responsibilities among fathers. The lives of the poor, all too often, are governed by the rhythms of tension and release that characterize the sexual experience of young single men. Because female sexuality, as it evolved over the millennia, is psychologically rooted in the bearing and nurturing of children, women have long horizons within their very bodies, glimpses of eternity within their wombs. Civilized society is dependent upon the submission of the short-term sexuality of young men to the extended maternal horizons of women. This is what happens in monogamous marriage; the man disciplines his sexuality and extends it into the future through the womb of a woman. . . .

An analysis of poverty that begins and ends with family structure and marital status would explain far more about the problem than most of the distributions of income, inequality, unemployment, education, IQ, race, sex, home ownership, location, discrimination, and all the other items usually multiply regressed and correlated on academic computers. But even an analysis of work and family would miss what is perhaps the most important of the principles of upward mobility under capitalism—namely faith. . . .

Faith in man, faith in the future, faith in the rising returns of giving, faith in the mutual benefits of trade, faith in the providence of God are all essential to successful capitalism. . . . In order to give without the assurance of return, in order to save without the certainty of future value, in order to work beyond the requirements of the job, one has to have confidence in a higher morality: a law of compensations beyond the immediate and distracting struggles of existence. . . .

Welfare now erodes work and family and thus keeps poor people poor. Accompanying welfare is an ideology—sustaining a whole system of federal and state bureaucracies—that also operates to destroy their faith. The ideology takes the form of false theories of discrimination and spurious claims of racism and sexism as the dominant forces in the lives of the poor. The bureaucracies are devoted to "equal opportunity" and "affirmative action." Together they compete with welfare in their pernicious influence on the poor—most especially the poor who happen to be black.

The closing circle, the resource crisis, the thermal threat, the nuclear peril, the "graying" of technology, the population advance, the famine factor, and whatever else is new in the perennial jeremiad of the rational budgeteer and actuary of our fate—all these conditions are themselves the mandate for capitalism. To overcome it is necessary to have faith, to recover the belief in chance and providence, in the ingenuity of free and God-fearing men.

This belief will allow us to see the best way of helping the poor, the way to understand the truths of equality before God that can only come from freedom and diversity on earth. It will lead us to abandon, above all, the idea that the human race can become self-sufficient, can separate itself from chance and fortune in a hubristic siege of rational resource management, income distribution, and futuristic planning. Our greatest and only resource is the miracle of human creativity in a relation of openness to the divine. It is a resource that above all we should deny neither to the poor, who can be the most open of all to the future, nor to the rich or excellent of individuals, who can lend leadership, imagination, and wealth to the cause of beneficent change.

31

RONALD REAGAN

Speech to the National Association of Evangelicals
March 1983

Reagan's 1980 campaign stressed anti-Soviet, anti-federal government themes rather than moral values. In 1983, however, he took a step toward his faith-based allies by addressing the convention of the National Association of Evangelicals. The NAE was an anticommunist, anti–big government umbrella organization that encompassed dozens of Protestant denominations with millions of adherents. Many were Pentecostals who manifested their devotion through faith healing, speaking in tongues, and other expressions of religious enthusiasm. By the 1980s many identified with the general views of the Moral Majority and—after a flirtation with Jimmy Carter, a Southern Baptist—with "family values" Republicans.

Reagan's NAE convention appearance seemed to validate, in evangelical eyes, their growing concern with social issues. It was also a tip of the Republican cap to the potential clout of a Christian Right that now reached well beyond Jerry Falwell, a dimming though still notable presence. Reagan's speech situated the struggle over abortion and prayer within the broader struggle against the Soviet Union, the "evil empire," the "focus of evil in the modern world." The Great Communicator's bellicose address resonated with the cultural militancy of his evangelical audience.

I want you to know that this administration is motivated by a political philosophy that sees the greatness of America in you, her people, and in your families, churches, neighborhoods, communities—the institutions that foster and nourish values like concern for others and respect for the rule of law under God.

Now, I don't have to tell you that this puts us in opposition to, or at least out of step with, a prevailing attitude of many who have turned to

Congressional Record, March 1983.

a modern-day secularism, discarding the tried and time-tested values upon which our very civilization is based. No matter how well intentioned, their value system is radically different from that of most Americans. And while they proclaim that they're freeing us from superstitions of the past, they've taken upon themselves the job of superintending us by government rule and regulation. Sometimes their voices are louder than ours, but they are not yet a majority....

Let me state the case as briefly and simply as I can. An organization of citizens, sincerely motivated and deeply concerned about the increase in illegitimate births and abortions involving girls well below the age of consent, some time ago established a nationwide network of clinics to offer help to these girls and, hopefully, alleviate this situation. Now, again, let me say, I do not fault their intent. However, in their well-intentioned effort, these clinics have decided to provide advice and birth control drugs and devices to underage girls without the knowledge of their parents....

Is all of Judeo-Christian tradition wrong? Are we to believe that something so sacred can be looked upon as a purely physical thing with no potential for emotional and psychological harm? And isn't it the parents' right to give counsel and advice to keep their children from making mistakes that may affect their entire lives? ...

More than a decade ago, a Supreme Court decision literally wiped off the books of 50 States statutes protecting the rights of unborn children. Abortion on demand now takes the lives of up to 1½ million unborn children a year. Human life legislation ending this tragedy will some day pass the Congress, and you and I must never rest until it does. Unless and until it can be proven that the unborn child is not a living entity, then its right to life, liberty, and the pursuit of happiness must be protected.

You may remember that when abortion on demand began, many, and, indeed, I'm sure many of you, warned that the practice would lead to a decline in respect for human life, that the philosophical premises used to justify abortion on demand would ultimately be used to justify other attacks on the sacredness of human life—infanticide or mercy killing. Tragically enough, those warnings proved all too true. Only last year a court permitted the death by starvation of a handicapped infant....

Recent legislation introduced in the Congress by Representative Henry Hyde of Illinois not only increases restrictions on publicly financed abortions, it also addresses this whole problem of infanticide. I urge the Congress to begin hearings and to adopt legislation that will

protect the right of life to all children, including the disabled or handicapped.

Now, I'm sure that you must get discouraged at times, but you've
done better than you know, perhaps. There's a great spiritual awakening in America, a renewal of the traditional values that have been the
bedrock of America's goodness and greatness.

One recent survey by a Washington-based research council concluded that Americans were far more religious than the people of
other nations; 95 percent of those surveyed expressed a belief in God
and a huge majority believed the Ten Commandments had real meaning in their lives. And another study has found that an overwhelming
majority of Americans disapprove of adultery, teenage sex, pornography, abortion, and hard drugs. And this same study showed a deep
reverence for the importance of family ties and religious belief.

I think the items that we've discussed here today must be a key
part of the Nation's political agenda. For the first time the Congress is
openly and seriously debating and dealing with the prayer and abortion issues—and that's enormous progress right there. I repeat:
America is in the midst of a spiritual awakening and a moral renewal.
And with your Biblical keynote, I say today, "Yes, let justice roll on like
a river, righteousness like a never-failing stream." . . .

And this brings me to my final point today. During my first press
conference as President, in answer to a direct question, I pointed out
that, as good Marxist-Leninists, the Soviet leaders have openly and
publicly declared that the only morality they recognize is that which
will further their cause, which is world revolution. I think I should
point out I was only quoting Lenin, their guiding spirit, who said in
1920 that they repudiate all morality that proceeds from supernatural
ideas—that's their name for religion—or ideas that are outside class
conceptions. Morality is entirely subordinate to the interests of class
war. And everything is moral that is necessary for the annihilation of
the old. . . .

They must be made to understand we will never compromise our
principles and standards. We will never give away our freedom. We
will never abandon our belief in God. And we will never stop searching
for a genuine peace. But we can assure none of these things America
stands for through the so-called nuclear freeze solutions proposed by
some. . . .

Yes, let us pray for the salvation of all of those who live in that totalitarian darkness—pray they will discover the joy of knowing God. But
until they do, let us be aware that while they preach the supremacy of

the state, declare its omnipotence over individual man, and predict its
eventual domination of all peoples on the Earth, they are the focus of
evil in the modern world. . . .

I believe we shall rise to the challenge. I believe that communism is
another sad, bizarre chapter in human history whose last pages even
now are being written. I believe this because the source of our
strength in the quest for human freedom is not material, but spiritual.
And because it knows no limitation, it must terrify and ultimately triumph over those who would enslave their fellow man.

32

J. A. DORN

Social Security:
Continuing Crisis or Real Reform?

1983

*Social Security presented a problem for conservatives. Opposed by Robert
Taft and many others as a costly giveaway that would sap individual initiative, the program became so popular that no practical politician,
including Nixon and Reagan, dared attack it directly. It also became
very large, touching virtually every American and disbursing billions of
dollars—the quintessential centralized New Deal program that conservatives abhorred.*

*It fell to the conservative movement's libertarian wing to develop
the lines of attack, which they began by way of the Cato Institute, a free-
market think tank funded by right-wing foundations. In 1983 Cato was a
major advocate for tax reduction, business deregulation, and the privatization of services, including Social Security. Economist J. A. Dorn, a
Cato vice president, compiled the first major set of justifications for privatization in 1983. Built on the work of the Austrian and Chicago
schools of economics, pieces of the study appeared in the* Cato Journal
and, as became standard practice, in briefing papers and talking points

J. A. Dorn, "Social Security: Continuing Crisis or Real Reform?" *Cato Journal*, 1983.

for Republican Congress and party spokespersons. Within twenty years Republican demands for Social Security "reform" had become so loud that even Democrats expected the system to be changed, if not eventually dismantled.

The opposition of the elderly to benefit cuts and the discontent of younger workers over the prospect of declining (or even negative) returns on their Social Security taxes threatens to create an increasing amount of intergenerational conflict. A realistic appraisal of the structural problems inherent in the Social Security system is necessary if meaningful reform is to be achieved and the intergenerational conflict resolved.

In order to consider the full range of reform proposals, the Cato Institute invited many of the nation's leading experts on Social Security to a two-day conference in Washington, D.C., June 6 and 7, 1983. The edited papers from that conference, along with A. Haeworth Robertson's congressional testimony on the National Commission's recommendations for Social Security reform, constitute this issue of the *Cato Journal*. The papers cover four main areas: the political economy of the Social Security system; options for reforming the system; the economic effects of Social Security; and strategy for dealing with the . . . problems associated with denationalizing [the Social Security system]. The following conclusions are noteworthy.

1. In analyzing Social Security, it is essential to consider the effects of property rights on incentives and individual behavior. The theory of public choice helps explain why the system has grown and why the public has resisted a more voluntary system of retirement insurance.

2. Social Security is ultimately a manifestation of the welfare state. Real reform, therefore, may require constitutional change that effectively limits the taxing and spending powers of government.

3. Advocates of real reform suggest, as the first step, separating the welfare and insurance components of the system. The insurance component could then be privatized and placed on a fully funded basis—an impossibility under government ownership and control. The private retirement system could also be made voluntary. Such a system would place responsibility on individual decision-makers and efficiently utilize existing knowledge to generate the best use of private savings. It would also reduce the encroachment on private property rights and strengthen freedom of contract.

4. Specific criteria should be considered in reforming the Social Security system. The system should foster economic efficiency (i.e., it should not distort economic behavior); sunk costs should be explicitly recognized and not be allowed to deter meaningful reform; the system should be free of political influences; and the system should be flexible, easily understood, and consistent with the principles of a free society. Adhering to these criteria will ensure the financial soundness of the system while promoting individual freedom and responsibility.

5. The existing pay-as-you-go system interferes with individual choice and distorts economic behavior in three ways. First, the system attenuates the freedom of workers to determine the optimal mix of savings and consumption for themselves (or the time path that they desire for consumption). Workers are forced to pay Social Security taxes—to redistribute income to the elderly—with the promise of future Social Security benefits. This process tends to depress private savings and investment. Second, Social Security interferes with the freedom of workers to determine the timing of retirement. The earnings test and other features of the system induce workers to retire earlier than they would in the absence of Social Security. Third, the payroll tax artificially increases the price of labor in relation to capital, causing a misallocation of resources.

6. Social Security affects both the intragenerational and intergenerational distribution of income. The 1983 amendments continue to redistribute income from high-income to low-income earners, from single persons to married couples, and from younger workers to the elderly retired. Most significant, the 1983 law imposes losses on all Social Security participants, with the greatest burden falling on the younger generation of workers.

7. The political barriers to privatizing the insurance component of Social Security are formidable, but not insurmountable. As the experience of Britain and other countries has demonstrated, it may be possible to move toward a system in which workers could allocate part of their payroll taxes to IRA-type investment accounts. This proportion could be increased over time until the transition to a private retirement system is complete.

. . . Further research, however, needs to be conducted on the economic effects of Social Security and on the political economy of privatization. We must also address the question of whether individuals have a right to social welfare and insurance. To answer this question, it will be necessary to go beyond economics and construct a consistent theory of rights. Developing such a theory could have a significant impact on the intellectual support for Social Security and could ultimately influence policy.

33

SOUTHERN BAPTIST CONVENTION

Resolution on Abortion

June 1984

Like southerners in other denominations, Southern Baptists separated from their northern brethren over slavery. Preaching biblical inerrancy, anti-Catholicism, separation of church and state, and congregational autonomy, they opposed gambling, drinking, dancing, and race mixing. But their true passion was calling lost souls to Christ. By the mid-twentieth century, the Southern Baptist Convention (SBC) was the country's largest, fastest-growing denomination, especially in the South, with some of its biggest congregations and television audiences.

Race mattered. Strom Thurmond, George Wallace, and Jesse Helms were Baptists, and Baptists organized many private white Christian academies after 1954. The SBC, however, passed few resolutions on any social issue until the 1970s, when it expressed alarm over crime rates and efforts to undermine parental rights and male prerogative. Abortion, too, was a concern, but unlike early anti-abortion activists, most of whom were Catholic, the SBC's first statement on the issue, in 1971, affirmed not only "a high view of life, including fetal life," but also the right to abortion "under such conditions as rape, incest, clear evidence of severe fetal deformity" and likely damage to the "emotional, mental and physical health of the mother."

A major shift occurred in 1980, when the Convention opposed taking the life of a "developing human being" except to save the mother's life and urged a constitutional amendment to that effect. A 1982 resolution called abortion the killing of 4,000 "pre-born persons" daily. The fullest expression of the new position came in 1984, which aligned Southern Baptists with Roman Catholicism and the Moral Majority.

Whereas, the Southern Baptist Convention, meeting in New Orleans in June 1982, clearly stated its opposition to abortion and called upon Southern Baptists to work for appropriate legislation and/or constitutional amendment which will prohibit abortions except to save the physical life of the mother; and

Whereas, in addition to legislative remedies for this national sin, it is incumbent that we encourage the woman who is considering abortion to think seriously about the grave significance of such action by presenting information to her about the unborn child in her womb, who is a living individual human being, and encourage her to consider alternatives to abortion; and

Whereas, Christlike love requires that such alternatives be made available.

Therefore, be it resolved, that the Southern Baptist Convention meeting in Kansas City, Missouri, June 12–14, 1984, encourage all of its institutions, cooperating churches, and members to work diligently to provide counseling, housing, and adoption placement services for unwed mothers with the specific intent of bringing them into a relationship with Jesus Christ and/or a sense of Christian responsibility; and

Be it further resolved, that we deplore the practice of performing abortions, as well as dispensing to minors without parental consent or even notification, contraceptive medications which have potentially dangerous side effects, and deplore also the use of tax funds for such activities; and

Be it further resolved, that we call upon all Southern Baptists to renew their commitment to support and work for legislation and/or constitutional amendment which will prohibit abortion except to save the physical life of the mother; and

Be it further resolved, that we encourage Southern Baptists to inquire whether or not their physicians perform abortions on demand or give referrals for abortions, and that we commend those of the medical profession who abstain from performing abortions or making abortion referrals; and

Be it finally resolved, that we urge our agencies and institutions to provide leadership for our cooperating churches and members, by preparing literature to take a clear and strong stand against abortion, and to inform and motivate our members to action to eliminate abortion on demand.

34

PRESIDENT'S COMMISSION ON PRIVATIZATION

Report on Privatization

March 18, 1988

A major drive to "privatize" government functions (sell or contract them to private businesses) developed in the 1970s and early 1980s. Free-market economists claimed that competition always provided goods and services more cheaply and efficiently than monopoly. Since government services were usually monopolies, they were by definition inefficient and costly. Private companies could also charge for or curtail services, thus avoiding deficits, a hallmark of inefficiency, which would reduce the need for public funding—and permit more tax cutting. If privatization could wean people from New Deal–type programs, as conservatives wanted, and undermine public employee unions, as Republicans wanted, then so much the better.

Prodded by economic libertarians and trying to reduce a swollen budget deficit, in 1987 Reagan appointed a thirteen-person commission to find government services to privatize. Consisting mainly of the busy heads of major corporations, the commission delegated most of the work to director Stephen Moore, a Heritage Foundation executive, Fellow of the Cato Institute, and architect of an important "flat tax" proposal on behalf of House Republicans. Many of the proposals and most of the argument in the Commission's Final Report were the handiwork of Cato and Heritage by way of Moore.

Privatization proved slower work than tax cuts. Voters sometimes equated privatization with elimination, and they wanted the programs. But the Reagan Commission was an effective step in the assault on government. The very notion of publicly funded, owned, and operated

Privatization: Toward a More Effective Government (Washington, D.C.: Government Printing Office, 1988).

*institutions and amenities—schools, parks, hospitals, museums, trans-
portation, communications, dams, even military operations—fell increasingly by the wayside.*

The President's Commission on Privatization was established on September 2, 1987, "to review the appropriate division of responsibilities
between the federal government and the private sector," and to iden-
tify those government programs that are not properly the responsibility of the federal government or that can be performed more
efficiently by the private sector. . . .

The following are summaries of the Commission's findings and recommendations in each area:

Low-Income Housing

Rather than financing new public housing construction, the government should provide housing subsidies to eligible low-income house-
holds in the form of vouchers enabling them to rent acceptable
housing in the private marketplace. To the greatest extent possible
existing public housing should either be sold to or managed by the
residents. By giving residents a larger stake in their own housing by
selling it to them, contracting with them to manage it, or by allowing
them discretion in choosing it through a voucher program, the long-
term quality of their housing will be improved at a lower cost per
household.

Housing Finance

The federal government should assume a more neutral position with
respect to direct housing finance programs (Farmers Home Administration, Government National Mortgage Association, Federal Home
Loan Mortgage Corporation, Federal National Mortgage Association,
Federal Housing Administration, and Veterans Administration). In
addition, the federal government should refocus the mortgage insurance activity of the Federal Housing Administration so that it does not
compete as directly with private mortgage insurers. Rather, it should
direct its efforts, as originally intended, toward home buyers who
have been turned down by private insurers. Similarly, the Federal
National Mortgage Association and, by extension, the Federal Home
Loan Mortgage Corporation, should not be allowed to compete on an

unfair basis, and thus should be fully privatized, including the elimination of all federal benefits and limitations. . . .

Air Traffic Control and Other FAA Functions

The FAA should continue to regulate the national airspace system for the foreseeable future for reasons of safety, public service, and efficiency. However, portions of that system can and should be considered for private operation or for contracting, when such options would improve air commerce. In this regard, the federal government should reduce its direct role in the development of airports, by encouraging each airport to develop its own sources of funding from the full range of beneficiaries of aviation services. In particular, the portion of national airport and airway expenditures borne by users should be increased. Airport operators should be allowed to charge peak-hour takeoff and landing fees to alleviate congestion, and to charge passenger facility fees as a means of generating revenues. The FAA should retain authority over the en route centers, but some center activities should be subject to contracting out. In addition, the FAA should move incrementally to a system of private airport traffic control towers, and should privatize its system of flight service stations and system maintenance services.

Educational Choice

The federal government should foster choice options, including the use of vouchers to achieve the nation's full range of educational goals. Congress should adopt policies to increase parental choice in education at the elementary and secondary levels just as it now fosters choice in higher education through GI Bill payments and Pell Grants. Private schools should be able to participate in federal programs providing educational choice to parents, but the federal government should remain sensitive to retaining the values represented by the public schools and should ensure that the full range of civil rights guaranteed by the Constitution is protected.

The federal government should encourage choice programs targeted to individuals in the lower percentiles of the current elementary and secondary student population. The schools are failing these children now, and alternatives beyond current programs should be explored. Finally, the Secretary of Education should use discretionary resources to conduct additional research on educational choice initiatives that might expand the range of educational options for children.

Postal Service

The private express statutes, which mandate the postal monopoly, should be repealed to allow competition in the provision of any and all postal services. The benefits conferred by competition, in terms of quality of service, cost efficiency, and the incentives for innovation, clearly outweigh the costs of transition to a free market. However, there must be a gradual phase-in period and compensation of postal employees for possible loss of benefit or earnings. The U.S. Postal Service should seek private sector involvement, with consideration given to selling it as an Employee Stock Ownership plan. As part of the phase-in process, the monopoly restrictions on the carriage of third-class mail and on rural delivery should be lifted immediately. Similarly, the restrictions on private delivery of urgent mail should be loosened and the prohibition on private use of letter boxes should be repealed immediately. At the same time, the Postal Service should more actively pursue contracting out opportunities in all its functions and ensure highest and best use of all its assets.

Contracting Out

The federal government should not compete with the private sector in the provision of commercially available goods and services. Contracting out through the competitive bidding process should be pursued more aggressively through the Executive Branch as a means to procure the same or better level of service at a reduced cost. . . .

MILITARY COMMISSARIES

Private sector businesses should participate in managing and operating military commissaries in the United States in order to achieve greater efficiency through competitive stimulus.

PRISONS

Contracting the administration of jails and prisons at the federal, state, and local levels could lead to improved, more efficient operation. Problems of liability and accountability should not be seen as posing insurmountable obstacles to contracting for the operation of confinement facilities, although Constitutional and legal requirements apply. Contracted facilities may also be required to meet American Correctional Association standards.

The Bureau of Prisons and the Immigration and Naturalization Service (INS), in cooperation with the appropriate government agencies, should prepare cost studies . . . comparing the cost of contracting with total government costs for administering existing facilities. In addition, the Bureau of Prison and the INS should be encouraged and authorized to pursue lease-purchase arrangements for the addition of new facilities and the Department of Justice should continue to give high priority to research on private sector involvement in corrections. . . .

AMTRAK

Private sector initiative in the provision of intercity passenger rail service should be encouraged. The federal government should adopt a multi-year plan to move Amtrak or major portions of its operations to the private sector, in conjunction with repealing Amtrak's exclusive rights to provide intercity rail service. As part of the multi-year plan, federal subsidies should be incrementally reduced, and a deadline should be set for the Department of Transportation to decide whether Amtrak or portions of its operations should be continued. Capital needs should be funded by the federal government only if the purchase can be justified as a means to reduce the federal subsidy and to facilitate the eventual transfer of Amtrak to the private sector with no additional commitment of federal funds, including government loan guarantees. At the same time, Amtrak should contract out operations wherever the level of service can be performed at an equal or improved level and cost savings would result—taking into consideration the interest of employees. It should charge states and other users the full costs associated with providing rail service and trackage rights. . . .

MEDICARE

Private sector competition, by means of vouchers, in the provision of health care financing (health insurance or HMOs) for the elderly can impart critically needed cost-containment incentives in this market and offer a broader choice of health plan options. The government should act to increase competition and private sector participation in health care financing under Medicare by encouraging the use of vouchers or capitated payments to purchase private health care financing. Since the private sector is naturally reluctant to assume greater risk without compensating benefits, some risk-sharing plan, such as the use of risk-corridors, should be considered in the implementation of any voucher system.

35

ANTONIN SCALIA

Opinion on the Juvenile Death Penalty

1988

Reagan appointed Antonin Scalia to the Supreme Court in 1986 in an effort to move the Court to the right. The judiciary was a long-standing thorn in the side of the conservatives. Thurmond and Wallace had railed against judicial tyranny; the Birchers tried to impeach Earl Warren, whose Court declared segregation unconstitutional; and churches attacked the Court over abortion and school prayer. Nixon's appointment of William Rehnquist, Reagan's of Antonin Scalia, and George H. W. Bush's of Clarence Thomas were designed to turn the tide. The Federalist Society, founded by Rehnquist in 1982 and dedicated to appointing conservative judges and restoring conservative principles, helped the process along.

The restoration of individual and social discipline was a major motive in this effort. Traditionalists doubted people's ability to control themselves without external authority, as did southern defenders of slavery and, later, segregation. The twentieth century modified these views, but Russell Kirk still considered faith, property, and families indispensable to order. Agnew blasted lax child-rearing, Schlafly the pampered "mommy" society, Reagan and Gilder the welfare state that destroyed personal initiative. People needed to be reared, induced, or forced to behave — or face the consequences. Antonin Scalia, soon to become a hero of the Right, was a textualist ("original intent" jurist) whose opinion in Thompson v. Oklahoma *reflected his view that the Constitution means what it says and that since the Framers were willing to execute minors, so should*

Thompson v. Oklahoma 487 U.S. 815 (1988).

*modern Americans. Justice Scalia's support for execution of the retarded
and life imprisonment for a third felony likewise reflected conservatism's
punitive claim that offenders should pay for their crimes regardless of the
circumstances.*

If the issue before us today were whether an automatic death penalty
for conviction of certain crimes could be extended to individuals
younger than 16 when they commit the crimes, thereby preventing
individualized consideration of their maturity and moral responsibility,
I would accept the plurality's conclusion that such a practice is
opposed by a national consensus, sufficiently uniform and of sufficiently long standing, to render it cruel and unusual punishment
within the meaning of the Eighth Amendment. We have already
decided as much, and more, in *Lockett v. Ohio*, 438 U.S. 586 (1978). I
might even agree with the plurality's conclusion if the question were
whether a person under 16 when he commits a crime can be deprived
of the benefit of a rebuttable presumption that he is not mature and
responsible enough to be punished as an adult. The question posed
here, however, is radically different from both of these. It is whether
there is a national consensus that no criminal so much as one day
under 16, after individuated consideration of his circumstances, including the overcoming of a presumption that he should not be tried as an
adult, can possibly be deemed mature and responsible enough to be
punished with death for any crime. Because there seems to me no
plausible basis for answering this last question in the affirmative, I
respectfully dissent. . . .

William Wayne Thompson is not a juvenile caught up in a legislative scheme that unthinkingly lumped him together with adults for
purposes of determining that death was an appropriate penalty for him
and for his crime. To the contrary, Oklahoma first gave careful consideration to whether, in light of his young age, he should be subjected to
the normal criminal system at all. That question having been
answered affirmatively, a jury then considered whether, despite his
young age, his maturity and moral responsibility were sufficiently
developed to justify the sentence of death. In upsetting this particular-
ized judgment on the basis of a constitutional absolute, the plurality
pronounces it to be a fundamental principle of our society that no one
who is as little as one day short of his 16th birthday can have sufficient maturity and moral responsibility to be subjected to capital pun-

ishment for any crime. As a sociological and moral conclusion, that is implausible; and it is doubly implausible as an interpretation of the United States Constitution.

The text of the Eighth Amendment, made applicable to the States by the Fourteenth, prohibits the imposition of "cruel and unusual punishments." The plurality does not attempt to maintain that this was originally understood to prohibit capital punishment for crimes committed by persons under the age of 16; the evidence is unusually clear and unequivocal that it was not.... The historical practice in this country conformed with the common law understanding that 15-year-olds were not categorically immune from commission of capital crimes. One scholar has documented 22 executions, between 1642 and 1899, for crimes committed under the age of 16 ...

Necessarily, therefore, the plurality seeks to rest its holding on the conclusion that Thompson's punishment as an adult is contrary to the "evolving standards of decency that mark the progress of a maturing society." ... Of course, the risk of assessing evolving standards is that it is all too easy to believe that evolution has culminated in one's own views. To avoid this danger, we have, when making such an assessment in prior cases, looked for objective signs of how today's society views a particular punishment.... It will rarely, if ever, be the case that the Members of this Court will have a better sense of the evolution in views of the American people than do their elected representatives.

It is thus significant that, only four years ago, in the Comprehensive Crime Control Act of 1984 ... Congress expressly addressed the effect of youth upon the imposition of criminal punishment, and changed the law in precisely the opposite direction from that which the plurality's perceived evolution in social attitudes would suggest: it lowered from 16 to 15 the age at which a juvenile's case can, "in the interest of justice," be transferred from juvenile court to Federal District Court, enabling him to be tried and punished as an adult.... Since there are federal death penalty statutes which have not been determined to be unconstitutional, adoption of this new legislation could at least theoretically result in the imposition of the death penalty upon a 15-year-old....

Turning to legislation at the state level, one observes the same trend of lowering rather than raising the age of juvenile criminal liability. As for the state status quo with respect to the death penalty in particular: The plurality chooses to "confine [its] attention" to the fact that all 18 of the States that establish a minimum age for capital punishment have chosen at least 16. But it is beyond me why an accurate analysis would not include within the computation the larger number of States (19) that have determined that no minimum age for capital punishment is appropriate, leaving that to be governed by their general rules for the age at which juveniles can be criminally responsible. A survey of state laws shows, in other words, that a majority of the States for which the issue exists (the rest do not have capital punishment) are of the view that death is not different insofar as the age of juvenile criminal responsibility is concerned. And the latter age, while presumed to be 16 in all the States, can, in virtually all the States, be less than 16 when individuated consideration of the particular case warrants it. Thus, what Oklahoma has done here is precisely what the majority of capital-punishment States would do. . . .

In sum, the statistics of executions demonstrate nothing except the fact that our society has always agreed that executions of 15-year-old criminals should be rare, and in more modern times has agreed that they (like all other executions) should be even rarer still. There is no rational basis for discerning in that a societal judgment that no one so much as a day under 16 can ever be mature and morally responsible enough to deserve that penalty; and there is no justification except our own predeliction for converting a statistical rarity of occurrence into an absolute constitutional ban. . . . One could readily run the same statistical argument with respect to other classes of defendants. Between 1930 and 1955, for example, 30 women were executed in the United States. Only three were executed between then and 1986—and none in the 22-year period between 1962 and 1984. Proportionately, the drop is as impressive as that which the plurality points to in 15-year-old executions. (From 30 in 25 years to 3 in the next 31 years, versus from 18 in 50 years to potentially 1—the present defendant—in the next 40 years.) Surely the conclusion is not that it is unconstitutional to impose capital punishment upon a woman. . . .

Having avoided any attempt to justify its holding on the basis of the original understanding of what was "cruel and unusual punishment," and having utterly failed in justifying its holding on the basis of "evolving standards of decency" evidenced by "the work product of state legislatures and sentencing juries," the plurality proceeds, in Part V of the opinion, to set forth its views regarding the desirability of ever imposing capital punishment for a murder committed by a 15-year-old. That discussion begins with the recitation of propositions upon which there is "broad agreement" within our society, namely, that "punishment should be directly related to the personal culpability of the criminal defendant," and that "adolescents as a class are less mature and responsible than adults." It soon proceeds, however, to the conclusion that "[g]iven the lesser culpability of the juvenile offender, the teenager's capacity for growth, and society's fiduciary obligations to its children," none of the rationales for the death penalty can apply to the execution of a 15-year-old criminal, so that it is "nothing more than the purposeless and needless imposition of pain and suffering." On this, as we have seen, there is assuredly not general agreement. Nonetheless, the plurality would make it one of the fundamental laws governing our society solely because it has an "abiding conviction. . . ."

36

WILLIAM G. LAFFER III

George Bush's Hidden Tax:
The Explosion in Regulation

1992

Deregulation was the third leg, along with tax cuts and privatization, of the conservative economic stool. All stemmed from the same principle: Taxes, government service, and regulations implied government economic intervention and therefore government decision making. History taught the Right that this would produce "creeping socialism," an expanded "welfare state," or, at the least, interference with capitalist markets and therefore inefficiency and loss of freedom. It often proved easier, in fact, to deregulate administratively than to go through Congress to reduce taxes or privatize services. Jimmy Carter began the process with airline deregulation in the 1970s. Reagan loosened laws relating to broadcasting, oil production, federal lands, and other areas. After Reagan, George H. W. Bush was a disappointment, as shown in this Heritage Foundation study by the son of Arthur Laffer, a Reagan-era advocate of lower taxes even at the expense of higher deficits.

Heritage was a logical sponsor of the study. Weyrich and Joseph Coors established the Foundation in 1973 in order to "formulate and promote

William G. Laffer III, "George Bush's Hidden Tax: The Explosion in Regulation." www .heritage.org/Research/Regulation/BG905.cfm.

*conservative public policies based on the principle of free enterprise, lim-
ited government, individual freedom, traditional American values, and
a strong national defense." Money soon flowed from conservative foundations, multinationals, and the Unification Church, publisher of the*
Washington Star. *By the 1990s Heritage was the largest and wealthiest
of the country's ideological think tanks—and its most influential.
Speaker of the House Newt Gingrich (R-GA) called Heritage "the most
far-reaching conservative organization in the country in the war of
ideas."*

America has experienced an enormous growth in regulation over the
last three years, due almost entirely to legislation signed by Bush, and
to the decisions of officials he has appointed. This burgeoning red
tape hinders the economy's recovery and jeopardizes future economic
progress. . . .

This new regulatory build-up is taking an increasing toll on the
economy. It is like a hidden tax. And just like a tax, regulation:

— raises the prices paid by consumers;
— lowers wages and increases unemployment;
— hurts the country's international competitiveness;
— increases uncertainty for businesses and reduces investment;
    and
— impairs innovation. . . .

Environmental regulation accounts for the largest share of the recent
explosion of regulations. Bush promised during the 1988 campaign to
support a new clean air bill, and he was instrumental in securing its
passage. Estimates of the cost of the legislation vary, but all are huge.
Murray Weidenbaum, former chairman of the Council of Economic
Advisors under Reagan and now Director of the Center for the Study
of American Business at Washington University in Saint Louis, estimates that the law "will cost an added $25–35 billion a year, over and
above the more than $100 billion [already] spent annually on all pollu-
tion controls." . . .*

Although described as a "civil rights" bill by its supporters, including President Bush, the Americans with Disabilities Act (ADA) does
much more than simply prohibit discrimination against the disabled. It

*Citations omitted.

also requires owners of private businesses, apartment buildings, restaurants, and stores to make—at their own expense—various physical modifications to their premises, such as widening doorways and installing wheelchair ramps, in order to accommodate the disabilities of current and potential employees, tenants, and customers. Likewise, hotels and auto rental companies must go to the extra expense of including wheelchair lifts on all their new pick-up vans. And similarly, public transit systems are required to install wheelchair lifts on all new buses. . . . In the case of many enterprises or places of employment in many parts of the country, there might be few or no disabled customers or workers currently facing significant obstacles. In these cases, forcing each business to spend thousands or even hundreds of thousands of dollars to comply with the letter of the law makes little economic sense, and in some cases may endanger the survival of the business. . . .

Ostensibly an attempt merely to restore civil rights law to where it stood before a series of Supreme Court decisions in 1988, the 1991 Civil Rights Act legislation radically changed federal employment discrimination law. It made it easier for employees to sue employers, harder for employers to defend themselves successfully—even when they are innocent of any actual discrimination—and more expensive for employers when they lose cases. . . .

The additional costs due to litigation and fines will act like a tax on employment. . . . It will cost the economy jobs, lower wages, and make American firms less competitive. . . .

When regulations are viewed as a whole rather than in isolation, they are seen to act as a hidden tax. This tax takes the form of such things as compliance expenditures, time lost due to paperwork requirements, delays in the processing and issuance of permits required by government, and attorney fees incurred in regulation-related litigation.

Just like any other tax, moreover, regulation imposes broad economic costs on Americans. Among the most important economic consequences:

> Regulation raises prices paid by consumers and thereby lowers living standards.

> Regulations impose substantial compliance costs which must be borne by someone. These costs are borne in part by businesses' employees and stockholders. To some extent, however businesses pass these costs on to their customers in the form of higher prices. . . .

Some regulations have a direct and immediate impact on wages and employment. The minimum wage law, federal labor laws, and federal civil rights laws, for example, all tend to increase the cost of employing workers and thereby decrease the levels of wages or employment, and sometimes both. Other regulations affect wages and employment indirectly, but just as significantly. Banking and environmental regulations, for example, both reduce the overall level of economic activity. . . .

Regulation increases uncertainty for business and reduces investment.

Regulations reduce the rate of return on investments made in the United States and encourage firms to move overseas. Moreover, the threat of future regulation adds to the economic uncertainty that businesses must face, and hence discourages long-term investment. By changing or reinterpreting the fine print of regulations, for example, government bureaucrats, the courts, or Congress itself can destroy the value of existing investments. Rather than risk making large investments that regulators might make worthless in the future, therefore, businesses have an incentive to shy away from large, long-term investments, and to seek instead shorter-term profits. . . .

Regulation discourages investment in the development of new technologies, manufacturing processes, and product designs. While this is true to some extent of all regulations and all kinds of innovation, certain particular regulations are especially destructive of particular kinds of innovation. For example, the 1962 amendments to the federal Food, Drug and Cosmetic Act significantly complicated the FDA drug approval process. According to several studies, this doubled the cost of developing drugs in the United States. . . .

The U.S. economy is being strangled by new regulation, much of which has come into being during George Bush's term of office. As a result, the total cost to the economy of state and federal regulation actually may now exceed the total cost of taxation.

37

JENNY WESTBERG

Abortion Drawings

1993

The base of the anti-abortion movement consisted of conservative churches, Protestant and Catholic, and Republican operatives, inside and beyond the pews and pulpits. It did not extend to independents or suburban moderates outside the South. Neither Reagan nor George H. W. Bush campaigned on the issue.

In 1993 Jenny Westberg, a pro-life Oregon housewife and sometime clinic protestor with cartooning experience, produced the following depictions of what happens to an advanced fetus during an abortion. Based on detailed medical instructions from a conference in Dallas on how to perform abortions, the drawings appeared in Life Advocate, *a small Portland magazine that had printed other anti-abortion cartoons by Westberg. The National Right to Life Committee and other large anti-abortion organizations immediately reproduced and distributed the cartoons, including to legislators and members of Congress.*

Although depictions of abortions had already appeared, they tended to be fuzzy, obscure, or simply too gruesome to comprehend. Westberg's clear, clinical drawings moved the anti-abortion movement well beyond the Christian Right. States reduced the time during a pregnancy when doctors could perform abortions. Congress eventually passed a Partial-Birth Abortion Ban Act barring abortion procedures that might cause the fetus pain, as Westberg's drawings seemed to suggest, rather than abortions after a particular point in pregnancy.

Life Advocate (1993), as reproduced in Cynthia Gorney, "Gambling with Abortion," *Harper's Magazine,* November 2004, 36–37.

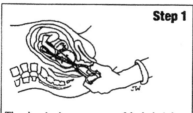

Step 1

The abortionist grasps one of the baby's legs with forceps.

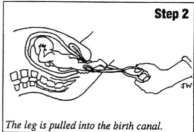

Step 2

The leg is pulled into the birth canal.

Step 3

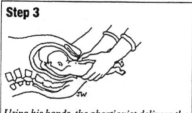

Using his hands, the abortionist delivers the baby's body. The head remains inside.

Step 4

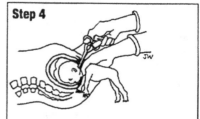

The abortionist forces scissors into the base of the baby's skull. He then opens the scissors to enlarge the hole.

Step 5

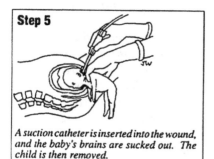

A suction catheter is inserted into the wound, and the baby's brains are sucked out. The child is then removed.

Courtesy of the National Right to Life Committee.

38

DAVID FRUM

From *Dead Right*

1994

Conservatives had to face the burning question of how to maintain social order and individual discipline in a country that was democratic, individualistic, and materialistic. This was a poor environment for the kind of right-wing traditionalism (prestigious military, stable ruling class, religion-infused state, outsized leaders) that had imposed order and discipline in other times and places. The search for alternatives was on: tough punishment, morality-based education, demanding churches, male authority, workplace discipline, stable families, and most of all the unfettered economic marketplace—the compulsions of capitalism itself.

The case for economic compulsion as ultimate discipline found exceptional expression in David Frum's Dead Right *(1994), a work that* The New York Times *called "the smartest book written from the inside about the American conservative movement." Frum, a Canadian, was a speechwriter for George W. Bush, an American Enterprise Institute Fellow,* National Review *columnist, and Federalist Society president.* The Wall Street Journal *acclaimed him as "one of the leading political commentators of his generation."*

Conservatism has not been entirely well served by geniality. It broadcasts wrong messages. Reagan's geniality misled his supporters into underestimating the resolution required of them if the frontiers of the state were to be rolled back. Reagan's manner was contrived to say, "Look, I wouldn't be doing any of this if any truly needy person anywhere in the country would suffer by it." When it later emerged that after all some needy persons had indeed suffered by some Reaganite measure, conservatives were left gasping. . . .

Any policy change in a nation of 235 million is going to produce losers. Compulsory airbags in cars will crush drivers' hands and wrists in a certain statistically predictable number of accidents. Pure water laws

---

David Frum, *Dead Right* (New York: New Republic Books, 1994), 186–88, 190–99, 201–4.

can shut down family farms that cannot afford fancy drainage techniques. Year-round daylight savings time forces rural children to walk to the bus stop in the dark where onrushing motorists may kill them. A Yiddish saying has it that "for instance isn't proof," and the ability to show that tighter eligibility for Social Security disability payments has impoverished Mr. Gonzales in Albuquerque does not prove that tighter eligibility is not, overall, more fair than slack eligibility. . . .

Redistributionism has formed and shaped our collective sense of justice so entirely that even the most defiant nonconformist, on honest self-examination, must confess to it. Here's one telltale sign. Think of the subtitle of William Bennett's 1992 book, *The De-valuing of America: The Struggle for Our Children and Our Culture*. What is the locution "our children" doing in Bennett's mouth? The phrase contains the thought that one's obligations to all the other children in the country are similar in nature to one's obligations to one's own; that a purely political bond — that between citizens of one nation — can resemble in some meaningful way the biological bond between parent and child. For people who are always trying to extend the reach of the political, this is an attractive claim to make. It comes naturally to Mario Cuomo, because Cuomo understands its radical implications. "They are not my children, perhaps. Perhaps they are not your children. But Jesse [Jackson] is right; they are our children and we should love them." Why is Bennett going along?

Twenty years ago, an economist named Sam Peltzman noticed that drivers who wore seatbelts, while suffering far fewer accidents than drivers who did not, inflicted far more. The safer the driver personally felt, the more carelessly he drove. The welfare state functions as a political safety belt, reducing the riskiness of all of our lives; and just as with real safety belts, there are what Peltzman called "feedback effects" from our newfound sense of personal security. Some of these effects are undoubtedly good. Unemployment insurance, by easing fears of job loss, does seem to relax workers' apprehensions about technological change. Other effects, however, are not good.

Consider the example of what ranks in conservative thinking as the most corrupted institution in American society: the university. Suppose that there were no student loans and very little of any other sort of state aid to higher education; imagine that every student (save those who could win a scholarship from the university itself) were paying the full cost of his or her own tuition and that the university had no sources of income other than tuition, alumni gifts, endowment income, and grants from governments and corporations for specific research projects. In such a world, the universities would not look at all like the schools that now enrage conservative critics of American higher education. The less motivated students, or those students seeking only, as one conservative academic puts it, to prove the negative point that they are not so idle and incompetent as to fail to get a B.A., would drop away. The students who remained, paying $1,000 or more per course, would become more discriminating consumers. Some demand for film studies, black studies, gay studies, and courses on the novels of Louis L'Amour would of course linger on—but in a cash-on-the-barrelhead university, the demand for such courses would be much reduced, and so, pretty quickly, would be the supply. Fewer faculty would be able to teach those courses; faculty who could teach nothing else would have to find new lines of work. . . .

American universities teach what they do for the same reason Polish factories used to turn out pairs of boots with two left feet: because an absence of consumer sovereignty enables them to get away with it. The factories make what pleases them. . . . With greater sacrifices demanded of the families of those who sought higher education, the proportion of Americans going on to university would shrink. That would in turn mean that state governments could no longer count on higher education to remedy the deficiencies of high school education. America turns out students the way General Motors used to turn out cars: slovenly and stupid assembly workers bang the doors on any old way they feel like, counting on a highly paid team of fixers at the end of the line to redo and repair their bungled work. If the refinishers were to go out of business, the high schools would have to be run like a Toyota line instead: the job would have to be done right the first time. . . .

If large-scale state aid to higher education had never been tried, the universities would be more wholesome places today; if massive aid ended tomorrow they would tend over time to become more wholesome; and so long as universities remain free of any need to earn a living by charging students the full cost of each and every course of study, they will continue to act as they act now. . . .

The same feedback effect drives the crisis of family breakdown. You can never reform welfare in a way that simultaneously encourages people to work and that provides them with a decent livelihood if they don't. . . . If welfare had never been enlarged in the mid-1960s, if a sixteen-year-old who got pregnant in 1993 had the same five unpleasant options she did in 1963—give up the child, get an abortion, drop out of school and take a job, beg her furious parents for help, or somehow persuade the father to marry her and take a job himself—isn't it probable, as Charles Murray contends, that today's sixteen-year-olds would be as unlikely to give birth out of wedlock as those of 1963 were? . . .

The welfare state has weakened family structures. That was what social programs were meant to do. The family used to be connected by its members' mutual responsibility for child-rearing, unemployment, sickness, old age, disability, and burial. A woman who gave birth outside of marriage was burdening her mother and father. A man who abandoned his children was abandoning his pension. But while strict mutual responsibility did a fair job of deterring illegitimacy and abandonment, it never succeeded very well at coping with illegitimacy and abandonment when they occurred. The welfare state was intended to replace those old family functions, and thus reduce the economic importance of the family—which, predictably, weakened the family's stability. . . .

It is not very realistic of conservatives to expect that the family can survive in its pre–Social Security form in a Social Security world. Affection is one of the most impermanent and weakest of human ties, but affection is now all that holds families together. Bill Bennett's search for "economic and social policies that support the two-parent family" is going to be disappointed. "Supporting the family" in Washington parlance is code for subsidies and welfare programs—family leave, day care—that is, for more of the forces in modern life that are subverting the family. Family leave and day care strike at the family's core economic logic, the sexual division of labor, depriving the family of the glue of mutual self-interest.

Conservatives who throw in the towel on issues like Social Security and Medicare and welfare in order to direct their full attention to "the culture" are attempting to preserve bourgeois values in a world arranged in such a way as to render those virtues at best unnecessary and at worst active nuisances. The project is not one that is very likely to succeed.

What are the bourgeois virtues anyway? The paramount ones are thrift, diligence, prudence, sobriety, fidelity, and orderliness. Compared to the military, saintly, and romantic virtues—zeal, courage, passion, love of beauty, pride, and indifference to worldly goods—it is not a very poetic list. But they are the virtues that settled America (combined, of course, with a canny eye for the quick buck), and they are the virtues whose ebbing conservatives mourn. The bourgeois virtues developed into an almost national cultural norm because they were essential to survival in a country that was, until the 1930s, simultaneously rich in opportunities and full of terrible dangers from which there was no protection except one's own resources and the help of friends and family. The opportunities remain, but the dangers have dwindled. Why be thrifty any longer when your old age and health care are provided for, no matter how profligately you act in your youth? Why be prudent when the state insures your bank deposits, replaces your flooded-out house, buys all the wheat you can grow, and rescues you when you stray into a foreign battle zone? Why be diligent when half your earnings are taken from you and given to the idle? Why be sober when the taxpayers run clinics to cure you of your drug habit as soon as it no longer amuses you? Why be faithful when there are no consequences at all to leaving your family in search of newer and more exciting pleasures? Why be neat and uncomplaining when squalor and whining are indictments not of you, but of society— and when the whinier and more squalid you are, the more society will pay to eradicate your problems? . . .

All of these changes have had the same effect: the emancipation of the individual appetite from the restrictions imposed on it by limited resources, or religious dread, or community disapproval, or the risk of disease or personal catastrophe. . . .

We cannot rescind the emancipation of appetite; but we can make its indulgence riskier by cancelling the welfare state's seductive invitation to misconduct.

39

SOUTHERN BAPTIST CONVENTION

Resolution on Homosexual Marriage

June 1996

The Southern Baptist Convention, still by far the largest Protestant denomination, completed its historic turn toward the right in the late twentieth century. Numerous resolutions opposed all kinds of legislation that permitted abortion, the Equal Rights Amendment, and the ordination of women. The SBC also opposed women in combat, which its members believed would undermine women's God-given role as nurturers and usurp men's responsibility as protectors and warriors. Other resolutions endorsed scriptural infallibility, scientific creationism, capital punishment and tax cuts, and opposed secular humanism and assisted suicide.

The 1996 resolution opposing homosexual marriage was one of the longest, most vehemently written in the denomination's history. It testified to the growing importance and politicization of this emotional issue everywhere, especially in the South. Other shorter resolutions were also startling. In 1988 the Convention redefined the "priesthood of the believer"—holy Baptist doctrine since the seventeenth century—to mean ministerial and organizational rather than individual prerogative, which strengthened the institutional church and its hierarchy at the expense of the worshipper. And in 1994 the Convention modified its ancient enmity to the Catholic Church to facilitate joint work against abortion, gay marriage, and pornography, and for the traditional family.

Whereas, in May 1993, the Hawaiian Supreme Court ruled that the state's exclusion of same-sex couples from marital status may be contrary to the Hawaiian state constitution because it amounts to invidious discrimination; and

Whereas, the Hawaiian Supreme Court has instructed the state of Hawaii to prove compelling state interests for limiting marriage to heterosexual couples; and

Whereas, the instructions of the Hawaiian Supreme Court shift the burden of proof from persons seeking to change existing law and places it instead on officers of the government who support norms of conduct long established in the Western legal tradition; and

Whereas, the compelling state interests standard is extraordinarily difficult to prove before a court already disposed to regard the exclusion of same-sex relationships from the definition of marriage as a matter of invidious discrimination, and therefore the state of Hawaii is soon likely to grant full legal status to the marriage of homosexual couples; and

Whereas, under the full faith and credit clause of the Constitution of the United States, any marriage performed in the state of Hawaii will, apart from the enactment of state-by-state exceptions or the enactment of a new and comprehensive federal law, have to be legally recognized in every other state; and

Whereas, homosexual couples from every other state are preparing to obtain marriage licenses in Hawaii and then to challenge the courts, legislatures and institutions in their home states to treat their same-sex relationship as having identical status to the recognition of marriage between a man and a woman; and

Whereas, challenging the exclusion of homosexual couples from the definition of marriage as sanctioned and protected by civil law is a strategy to appropriate the moral capital of marriage in order to enforce acceptance of homosexual conduct and homosexual desires in the public arenas of American life; and

Whereas, there is much scientific evidence showing that homosexual attractions are pathological, abnormal, and mostly if not entirely a matter of external influence, learned behavior, acquired taste and personal choice; and, although there have been speculations, no conclusive scientific evidence has been found to support claims that homosexual attractions are biologically fixed and irreversible; and

Whereas, even should a biological link with homosexuality be discovered, it could not settle the morality of homosexual behavior, and could not serve to justify, much less require, any society to grant the status of marriage to homosexual couples; and

Whereas, God, who is both Moral Ruler of the Universe and the Creator of all that is, and who knows and understands the physical and psychological composition of all and every human life better than any human scientist will ever know it, has stated in Scripture that homosexual conduct is always a gross abomination for all human beings, both men and women, in all circumstances, without exception (Lev. 18:22 and 20:13); and

Whereas, God makes it clear in Scripture that even desire to engage in a homosexual sexual relationship is always sinful, impure, degrading, shameful, unnatural, indecent and perverted (Rom. 1:24-27), so any effort to extend the meaning of marriage in order to sanction the satisfaction of such desire must also be in every case sinful, impure, degrading, shameful, unnatural, indecent and perverted; and

Whereas, God by saying their blood will be on their own heads (Lev. 20:13) has explicitly ruled out any effort by homosexual couples to justify their behavior, or to claim their homosexual relationship deserves protected legal status, by shifting blame or responsibility for their same-sex relationship to the Creator who made them; and

Whereas, marriage is God's idea established in the order of creation to be a permanent union of one man with one woman (Gen. 1:28, and 2:24), and marriage is therefore first and foremost a divine institution (Mat. 19:6) and only secondarily a cultural and civil institution; and

Whereas, Jesus reaffirmed the origin of marriage in the order of creation and declared marriage to be a sacred, monogamous and life-long institution joining one man with one woman (Matt. 19:4-6); and

Whereas, any action by the government giving homosexual unions the legal status of marriage denies the fundamental immorality of homosexual behavior and causes the government of any nation so doing to jeopardize seriously the favor of Almighty God on whom the security, welfare, and stability of every nation, even Gentile nations (Lev. 18:24-25, 28; Ps. 2; Am. 1:3, 6, 9, 11, 13; Isa. 13-21), ultimately depends; and

Whereas, separating marriage from the complementary union of male and female trivializes the concept of marriage in the laws, public policies, educational systems, and other institutions of society; and

Whereas, only the marriage of male and female serves to tame the impulses of self-centered individuals by inter-generational obligations and commitments; and

Whereas, failure in the courts and institutions of civil law to recognize the unique importance of heterosexual family units, by granting moral equivalence to the idea of same-sex relationships, will surely and very seriously undercut the formation of stable heterosexual family units in future generations; and

Whereas, the future of the United States of America will be placed at risk because no society can survive that does not recognize, protect, defend the unique importance of heterosexual marriage to its own health and stability; and

Whereas, the legal recognition of homosexual marriage carries the potential use of force, a force that will likely be turned against those who do not or cannot accept the moral equivalence of homosexual marriages; and

Whereas, the enforcement of marriage laws, standards of educational instruction in schools, and the regulation of fair business practices will be adjusted to require public recognition of homosexual marriages, and this adjustment will certainly undermine, and may even restrain, the public communication, influence, and independence of individuals, groups and institutions who believe and teach that homosexual marriage is immoral in both concept and practice; and

Whereas, legalizing homosexual marriage will force public schools to teach the acceptability of homosexual marriage and will likely lead to laws requiring that businesses remove distinctions between homosexual and heterosexual relationships in the way they treat marriage benefit for their employees; and

Whereas, legalizing homosexual marriage raises the specter of new laws and policies intended to marginalize, privatize, or silence the social and moral influence of parents and churches which teach that homosexual marriage is wrong or that heterosexual marriage is morally superior; now, therefore,

Be it resolved, that we, the messengers of the one hundred thirty-ninth meeting of the Southern Baptist Convention assembled in New Orleans, Louisiana, June 11–13, 1996, do clearly and steadfastly oppose the legalization of homosexual marriage by the state of Hawaii, or by any other state, or by the United States of America; and

Be it further resolved, that we affirm the Bible's teaching that promotion of homosexual conduct and relationships by any society, including action by the governments to sanction and legitimize homosexual relationships by the legalization of homosexual marriages, is an abominable sin calling for God's swift judgment upon any such society (Lev. 18:22, 28; Isa. 3.9);

Be it further resolved, that we commit ourselves to pray faithfully against the legalization of homosexual marriages in American law, and to preach and teach the truth concerning what the Bible says about homosexuality, homosexual conduct, and the institution of marriage, and against the foolishness, danger, and moral wickedness of any government action to accept, sanction, approve, protect, or promote homosexual marriage, and. . . .

Be it finally resolved, that because any law, or any policy or regulation supporting a law, that legalizes homosexual marriage is and must be completely and thoroughly wicked according to God's standards revealed in the Bible, we do most solemnly pledge our decision never to recognize the moral legitimacy of any such law, policy, or regulation, and we affirm that, whatever the stakes (Dan. 3:17-18), we will never conform to or obey (Acts 4:19) anything required by any governing body to implement, impose, or act upon any such law. So help us God.

40

RANDY TATE

Middle-Class Families Need a Flat Tax

1999

Conservatives never cared for the modern U.S. system of progressive taxation, which took a greater percentage of high incomes than of low incomes on the principle of "ability to pay." Until late in the century they generally demanded simply "lower" taxes rather than a wholly new tax system. In the 1970s, however, business investment flagged, which triggered a long-term lobbying campaign from business organizations for lower taxes on corporations and the wealthy, asserting that this would spur capital formation and improve global competitiveness. Meanwhile, conservative think tanks generated studies that made the same point: Low upper-income taxes would benefit everyone. Moreover, inflation was gradually kicking millions of ordinary voters into the higher tax brackets that were subject to progressive rates, making them susceptible to appeals for lower levies on high income. If flat rates benefited Republican constituencies, so much the better.

Flat-tax arguments worried conservatives who were concerned about budget deficits, and Republicans who were nervous about appearing too partial to the rich. But by the 1990s the concept had gained enough traction that Steve Forbes, a scion of the Forbes publishing family, could seek the Republican presidential nomination as a single-issue flat-taxer. His failed campaign breathed additional life into flat-tax thinking.

Randy Tate continued flat-tax advocacy for the Heritage Foundation in the wake of the Forbes campaign. A former member of Congress (R-WA), an ally of Republican Speaker Newt Gingrich, and executive director of the Christian Coalition — the successor to Falwell's Moral Majority — Tate's work and career showed the powerful continuing synergies among think tanks, the Christian Right, and the Republican party.

Adapted from Randy Tate's essay in the Heritage Foundation, *The IRS v. The People: Time for Real Tax Reform.*

America is currently enjoying a remarkable economic boom, characterized by low unemployment, low inflation, and almost weekly new stock market highs. More and more federal budget estimates are predicting a tremendous federal budget surplus over the next 10 years. But unless we demand and implement profound tax reform now, Washington bureaucrats and special interests will devise countless ways to spend the surplus.

Economic growth and prosperity cannot be measured just in terms of the gross national product, the Dow Jones average, and per capita income. I measure it in terms of the quality of life of average, hardworking families. Do both parents have to hold down full-time jobs merely to make ends meet? Are they able to take time off for family vacations? Are they free to arrive home at a decent hour for family dinner, or make time for their children's soccer games and school plays? As long as the federal government's tax policies prove more menacing than sensitive to America's families, real reform will still be needed.

I believe we should consider a simple, fair system that taxes income only one time and at one low rate—in short, a flat tax. Much of the rhetoric against the flat tax dismisses it as a gimmick for the rich, but the reality shows it could be some of the best news for hard-working American families since the microwave oven and the minivan. . . .

Some have objected that the flat tax treats the rich, middle-class, and poor alike—but that is precisely the point. The key to its fairness lies in the fact that in taxing people at the same equal rate, it will require those with means to pay a higher amount. The fabulously wealthy movie star or professional athlete who makes one thousand times as much money as the local plumber will pay one thousand times as much in taxes.

An additional benefit of a single-tax rate is that it will eliminate the insidious "marriage penalty," which taxes married couples at a higher rate than if the man and woman filed singly as individuals. At a time when family breakups are all too common, tax policy should place government on the side of America's families. It's their money and a government that truly supports families will let them keep it.

But a flat tax does more than simply hand a windfall tax cut to American families—it encourages economic growth. By taxing income only once (unlike the current system, which taxes income when we make it and again when we save it and earn interest), a flat tax encourages savings and investment. Small family businesses will have incentives to invest on the basis of what makes the most financial sense, not what constitutes the best tax write-off. This, in turn, will stimulate productivity and lead to higher wages and better economic health for all Americans.

I consider tax policy merely one component of a strong and virtuous society. Vibrant democracy, individual liberties, healthy families, robust religious institutions, and the rule of law all contribute to a strong America. But to the extent that our current tax system violates the basic principles of fairness, efficiency and liberty, it also undercuts rather than reinforces those other values and institutions that sustain our nation.

Cynics and liberals who dismiss demands for lower taxes and economic growth as appeals to greed seem to operate from the presumption that the federal government has the right to confiscate money from America's families, and it is only government benevolence that permits us to keep some of what we earn. I operate from a different presumption. The money that America's families work hard to earn is theirs by right, and it is only through the consent of the people that governments are authorized to collect taxes fairly, efficiently and responsibly. That's not greed—that's freedom.

41

TIM LaHAYE

Anti-Christ Philosophy Already Controls America and Europe

September 1999

Tim LaHaye was a California evangelical, a charter director of the Moral Majority, a cofounder (with his wife Beverly) of Family America, a Washington lobby, and the author of The Unhappy Gays *(1978), a pioneer antigay work. In* The Battle for the Mind *(1980), he identified "secular humanism" and liberals as the enemy of Christian America and*

Tim LaHaye, "Anti-Christ Philosophy Already Controls America and Europe," *Tim LaHaye's Perspective*, September 2004.

targeted "that man" Jimmy Carter (echoing what Republicans called FDR) for defeat. LaHaye mobilized Christian Right voters for Reagan via the American Coalition for Traditional Values, which received funds from Reagan's campaign, televangelists, and the Unification Church. He later wrote the Left Behind series of best-selling novels, which dealt in gruesome detail with the "rapture" predicted in the book of Revelation that would lift Christians to heaven and consign sinners to hell.

LaHaye shared the pro-family politics of his wife, Beverly, the head of Concerned Women for America, which mobilized Christian women to fight against communism, feminism, homosexuality, and other anti-family forces. His conservatism extended to foreign affairs, as in this searing attack on the UN. This reflected an anti–world government strain common in conservative thought since the days of Taft and Robert Welch, and more recently expressed in Pat Robertson's The New World Order *(1991). Some religious conservatives rejected LaHaye's emphasis on the coming "rapture," but there was little disagreement about the iniquity of the United Nations.*

All thinking people in America realize an anti-Christian, anti-moral, and anti-American philosophy permeates this country and the world. It dominates the public school system from kindergarten through graduate school. It controls the media from the daily print press to popular magazines (from porno to mainline), the six major TV networks, most of all cable TV; it dominates the entertainment industry, and it elects a predominance of liberals to both parties in our national government.

This alien philosophy does not come from the Bible, but is antithetical to it. In this country it flies under the banner of "liberalism," but in reality it is atheistic socialism at best and Marxism at worst. If those who hold this philosophy were honest and admitted publicly they were hostile to God, His Son Jesus Christ, moral values and true freedom for all individuals, they would be voted out of office in three quarters of the congressional districts and states in our country. Instead, they use the title "liberal" to define themselves and include the ACLU (the most harmful organization in American history), unions like the NEA (the largest teachers' union in the country), and thousands of other "liberal" organizations to destroy the Biblical principles this country was founded on and replace them with freedom from responsibility. These actions always lead to anarchy.

Anyone who takes the time to study the very effective workings of these "liberal" organizations will find they despise the mention of God (except in blasphemy), they disparage the name and people of Jesus Christ (easily the most influential person in all of human history), and they defame the moral values of Scripture (like virtue, honesty, and reverence). Instead, they advocate promiscuity by providing radically explicit sex education and providing condoms to minors, disregarding the concerns of the parents. They advocate homosexuality and demand that such sodomites be permitted to teach our young people. Abortion on demand is their way of coping with the unfortunate results of promiscuity, but they expect government to supply the money for research to overcome the sexually transmitted diseases that result from ignoring Biblical morality. Yet, these socialist communists who masquerade as "liberals" or "moderates" repeatedly condemn the Christian community for "imposing" our moral values on them, while raising our taxes to pay for the human tragedies that result from their anti-moral, government encouraged, libertine policies. . . .

The purchase of the 1996 election of the United States for Bill Clinton by the Chinese communists (which has been downplayed or ignored by our socialistic Marxist loving media) has resulted in the most corrupt administration in American history. Our current leaders see nothing wrong with betraying our national security secrets to their socialist Marxist friends whose world government policies they share.

All of which highlights the importance of the U.S. elections in the year 2000. Have you noticed how the socialist Marxist media, unions, and liberal politicos are gearing up for this election? They know that he who controls the appointing of the next three Supreme Court justices will influence the philosophy of the United States for the next twenty-five years. This may make it the most significant election in our lifetime.

We are the only nation that can halt the socialist Marxist enthronement of the UN as THE GLOBAL GOVERNMENT of the world, but it will require a conservative administration and Supreme Court committed to judicially interpreting our nation's laws that were originally based on moral Biblical principles.

Obviously, all it would take for the world government of socialistic Marxism to dominate this world with more anti-Christian, anti-moral values is the rapture of all Christians and the appearance of "the Man of Sin" who for seven years will "do his will." The signs of such a possibility are more apparent than they have ever been before. . . .

Can you even imagine what our world would be like culturally and socially if all the Christians were snatched out of this world? Suddenly there would be no one to champion the cause of the unborn, or oppose Planned Parenthood's promotion of sexual promiscuity and abortion in the public school, or government corruption or laws against gambling, drugs, homosexuality, pornography, and the list goes on. Bear in mind, these sins are already being advocated at government expense in the model nation in the world, the country that is called "the last best hope of mankind." . . .

If sixty million or so Christians were suddenly removed from this earth, leaving it without any morally "restraining" influence, how long do you think it would take for the other 200 million to turn this entire nation into Woodstock 2000—every day, everywhere? Let's face it, the Antichrist's philosophy is already here. And the only "restraining" influence are packing their bags because soon there will be "a shout from heaven" and we are out of here. I sure hope you are ready!

42

GEORGE W. BUSH

Nomination Acceptance Speech

2000

George W. Bush's 2000 presidential victory over a well-financed centrist Democrat showed the power of the conservative movement. Lacking Reagan's voice and stage presence and possessing wealth and connections that could have alienated working-class voters, he compensated by adopting a folksy Texas manner that played well in culturally conservative regions. His aggressive assertion of modern Republican themes excited party loyalists.

Bush's appeals for tax cuts were popular everywhere, including the two industrial states he won: Indiana and Ohio. His true strength, however, was in "heartland" states where gun ownership and the Christian Right were forces, and in the South, where an appearance at South Carolina's segregated, homophobic, evangelical Bob Jones University paid dividends. He was the first presidential contender to carry the evangelical vote overwhelmingly. He also won 70 percent of the southern white vote—80 percent in the old Thurmond/Goldwater/Wallace Deep South—and carried every southern state.

A loser in the popular national vote, Bush was nevertheless within reach of an electoral majority. The problem was Florida, with voting irregularities and a total too close to call. A recount was ordered that might have given the state, and the White House, to the Democrats, but it was not to be. After a series of challenges, the U.S. Supreme Court overruled a Florida court and halted the recount. The five judges who ruled in Bush's favor were all Republican appointees—one by Nixon, three by Reagan, and one by Bush's father. This triumph was eloquent testimony to the successful labors of two generations of American conservatives.

This administration had its moment.

They had their chance. They have not led. We will.

This generation was given the gift of the best education in American history. Yet we do not share that gift with everyone. Seven of ten fourth-graders in our highest poverty schools cannot read a single children's book.

And still this administration continues on the same old path with the same old programs—while millions are trapped in schools where violence is common and learning is rare.

This administration had its chance. They have not led. We will.

America has a strong economy and a surplus. We have the public resources and the public will—even the bipartisan opportunities—to strengthen Social Security and repair Medicare.

But this administration—during eight years of increasing need—did nothing.

They had their moment. They have not led. We will.

Our generation has a chance to reclaim some essential values—to show we have grown up before we grow old.

But when the moment for leadership came, this administration did not teach our children, it disillusioned them.

They had their chance. They have not led. We will . . .

Social Security has been called the "third rail of American politics"—the one you're not supposed to touch because it shocks you.

But, if you don't touch it, you can't fix it. And I intend to fix it.

To seniors in this country . . . You earned your benefits, you made your plans, and President George W. Bush will keep the promise of Social Security . . . no changes, no reductions, no way.

Our opponents will say otherwise. This is their last, parting ploy, and don't believe a word of it.

Now is the time for Republicans and Democrats to end the politics of fear and save Social Security, together.

For younger workers, we will give you the option—your choice— to put a part of your payroll taxes into sound, responsible investments.

This will mean a higher return on your money, and, over 30 or 40 years, a nest egg to help your retirement, or pass along to your children.

When this money is in your name, in your account, it's not just a program, it's your property.

Now is the time to give American workers security and independence that no politician can ever take away. . . .

My administration will give taxpayers new incentives to donate to charity, encourage after-school programs that build character, and support mentoring groups that shape and save young lives. . . .

Most of all, we must teach our children the values that defeat violence. I will lead our nation toward a culture that values life—the life of the elderly and the sick, the life of the young, and the life of the unborn. I know good people disagree on this issue, but surely we can agree on ways to value life by promoting adoption and parental notification, and when Congress sends me a bill against partial-birth abortion, I will sign it into law. . . .

Americans live on the sunrise side of mountain.

The night is passing.

And we are ready for the day to come.

Thank you. And God bless you.

A Chronology of the Conservative Movement (1947–2000)

1947   Congress passes the Taft-Hartley Act over President Truman's veto.

1948   Democratic party convention endorses strong civil rights plank. Southern Democrats bolt party over race issues and form States' Rights ("Dixiecrat") party; presidential candidate Strom Thurmond (South Carolina) wins thirty-nine Deep South electoral votes.

1949   USSR detonates atomic bomb, destroying United States' atomic monopoly.

        Chinese Communists defeat United States' Nationalist allies and take control of mainland China.

1950   Senator Joseph McCarthy launches investigation of "twenty years" of Democratic treason.

1951   Truman relieves General Douglas MacArthur of command in Korea.

1952   Eisenhower/Nixon ticket carries four southern states with fifty-seven electoral votes in landslide victory; first Republican triumph since 1928.

1954   Supreme Court strikes down the doctrine of "separate but equal" in *Brown v. Board of Education*.

1955   *National Review* launched.

1956   United States fails to support Hungarian anti-Soviet uprising.

1958   John Birch Society founded.

1960   Young Americans for Freedom founded.

        Barry Goldwater publishes *The Conscience of a Conservative*.

        John Tower becomes first Republican elected from Texas since Reconstruction.

1963 John F. Kennedy and NAACP official Medgar Evers assassinated.

1964 Strom Thurmond formally joins Republican party.

Barry Goldwater wins Republican presidential nomination, loses election to Lyndon Johnson but carries Deep South and runs well in West.

1965 President Johnson signs the Voting Rights Act; authorizes massive military buildup in Vietnam.

Race riot in Watts in Los Angeles; many others follow in next three years.

American Conservative Union, organized by Goldwater operatives, becomes first ultraconservative political lobby.

Richard V. Viguerie Company formed, revolutionizing conservative direct-mail fund-raising.

1966 Ronald Reagan elected governor of California after campaigning against antiwar and civil rights protests.

1968 Robert Kennedy and Martin Luther King Jr. assassinated.

Richard M. Nixon wins presidency, carrying five southern states.

George Wallace bolts Democratic party, gets 13 percent of the vote and carries five Deep South states; of the former Confederate states, Democrats carry only Texas, Lyndon Johnson's home state.

1972 Third-party conservative Wallace crippled in attempted assassination.

Nixon reelected, carries forty-nine states, including every southern state.

Business Roundtable organized.

Jesse Helms, hardline Republican conservative, elected to the Senate from North Carolina.

Nixon appoints William Rehnquist to Supreme Court.

Phyllis Schlafly organizes STOP ERA (later Eagle Forum).

1973 Supreme Court declares abortion to be a fundamental right in *Roe v. Wade.*

Heritage Foundation founded.

1974 Committee for the Survival of a Free Congress formed by Paul Weyrich.

Nixon resigns from the presidency amid Watergate scandal.

National Rifle Association establishes lobbying arm, moves to absolutist Second Amendment right to bear arms.

1975   National Conservative Political Action Committee founded; most powerful early right-wing political action committee.

Tax revolt flares in states and towns.

1976   Committee on the Present Danger formed to attack U.S. military weakness.

1977   Cato Institute founded.

Focus on the Family founded by James Dobson.

1978   Conservatives defeat AFL-CIO–backed Labor Law Reform Bill.

Conservative Republicans mobilize against the Panama Canal Treaty Bill.

Newt Gingrich, right-wing Georgia Republican, elected to the House; conservatives successfully target key congressional Democrats in fall elections.

1979   Moral Majority founded by Rev. Jerry Falwell.

Concerned Women of America founded by Beverly LaHaye.

1980   Ronald Reagan elected president, winning 51 percent of the vote; carries ten of eleven southern states with 118 electoral votes, 25 percent of Republican total.

Republicans elect thirty-three representatives and twelve senators, taking control of the upper chamber for the first time since 1954.

1981   Reagan fires air traffic controllers involved in the PATCO strike, abolishes controllers' union.

Congress passes Reagan proposal to slash top income tax rate.

Reagan names Sandra Day O'Connor to Supreme Court.

1982   Federalist Society organized to promote conservative legal principles and urge the appointment of conservative judges.

1983   Reagan orders invasion of Grenada.

Reagan attends convention of National Association of Evangelicals.

1984   Reagan wins landslide reelection, carries forty-nine states, including every southern state.

Southern Baptists pass resolution calling abortion "mass murder."

Vatican calls homosexuality a grave sin.

1986   Congress passes Reagan proposal to cut top income tax rate again.

Reagan names Antonin Scalia to Supreme Court and William Rehnquist to become Chief Justice.

1987   Senate rejects right-wing Reagan Supreme Court nominee Robert Bork; approves Anthony Kennedy instead.

1988   George H. W. Bush carries forty-two states in the presidential election, including entire South.

1989   Pat Robertson founds the Christian Coalition, naming Ralph Reed as its head.

Iron Curtain falls, USSR begins dissolution.

1991   Bush appoints Clarence Thomas to Supreme Court.

1994   Newt Gingrich unveils his Contract for America.

Republicans take control of both House and Senate for first time in forty years.

1995   Rev. Tim LaHaye publishes the first book in his soon-to-be best-selling Left Behind series.

1996   Southern Baptists pass resolution opposing homosexuality.

Bill Clinton signs bill passed by Republican Congress cutting welfare.

1998   Republican-controlled House votes to impeach President Clinton for perjury and obstruction of justice; Senate fails to convict.

2000   George W. Bush (R-TX) wins tight presidential election when the Supreme Court halts a recount in Florida; wins 155 southern electoral votes, over half the Republican total.

Questions for Consideration

1. Why, according to these documents, have some conservatives opposed a strong central government except in foreign policy? Have their reasons changed over time?

2. Why was religion less important in the early years of conservatism than it later became?

3. How have pro-life activists and traditional tax cutters found common ground in the conservative movement?

4. Which five documents in this collection seem most important in explaining the basic beliefs and goals of the conservative movement?

5. Which documents seem to have been the most influential in furthering the conservative cause?

6. Why has the South been of such critical long-term importance in the rise of conservatism? Has its importance shifted over time?

7. During the 1970s the conservatives brought a number of single-issue movements into the fold, including opponents of gun control, the Equal Rights Amendment, higher taxes, welfare payments, and affirmative action. What, if anything, did these movements have in common? What common denominators, if any, do the documents reveal?

8. Liberals have criticized the conservative movement for its underrepresentation of women and minorities. Do the documents support this criticism? If so, does that seem to be a consequence of the nature of conservatism itself?

9. Three political heroes of the Right were Barry Goldwater, Ronald Reagan, and George W. Bush. Compare and contrast their appeal and views, and explain their similarities and differences. Compare and contrast these conservative Republicans with ex-Democratic conservatives such as Strom Thurmond and George Wallace. Have liberals had comparable heroes?

10. How important, on the evidence of the record, was race in the forming of modern conservatism? Was it more important than gender? More important than class? Than region? Than patriotism? Than faith?

11. What factors do you think might explain the dramatic policy shifts of the Southern Baptist Convention?

12. What was the single biggest obstacle conservatives thought they faced in building their movement and gaining power? Were they correct?

13. Conservatives have been described as "policy critical" but "system supportive"—wanting, in other words, to change government policies and leaders but not the American system as a whole. Given the documentary record, does this seem an accurate appraisal?

14. Conservatives have been described as promoting "strong father" leadership and policies—decisive, protective, demanding, in control—as opposed to "caring mother" liberals. Do the documents support this kind of interpretation?

15. Conservatives have been described as having wealth redistribution upward as a constant long-term goal, with other concerns—religion, race, guns, and so forth—playing support roles. Do the documents support this kind of interpretation?

Selected Bibliography

OVERVIEWS

Ansell, Amy E., ed. *Unraveling the Right: The New Conservativism in American Thought and Politics.* Boulder, Colo.: Westview Press, 1998.

Brennan, Mary C. *Turning Right in the Sixties: The Conservative Capture of the GOP.* Chapel Hill: University of North Carolina Press, 1995.

Carter, Dan T. *From George Wallace to Newt Gingrich: Race in the Conservative Counterrevolution, 1963–1994.* Baton Rouge and London: Louisiana State University Press, 1996.

Crawford, Alan. *Thunder on the Right.* New York: Pantheon Books, 1980.

Diamond, Sara. *Roads to Dominion: Right-Wing Movements and Political Power in the United States.* New York: The Guilford Press, 1995.

———. *Not by Politics Alone: The Enduring Influence of the Christian Right.* New York: The Guilford Press, 1998.

Edwards, Lee. *The Conservative Revolution: The Movement That Remade America.* New York: The Free Press, 1999.

Hardisty, Jean. *Mobilizing Resentment: Conservative Resurgence from the John Birch Society to the Promise Keepers.* Boston: Beacon Press, 1999.

Hayward, Steven. *The Age of Reagan: The Fall of the Old Liberal Order, 1964–1980.* Roseville, Calif.: Forum/Prima, 2001.

Himmelstein, Jerome. *To the Right: The Transformation of American Conservatism.* Berkeley: University of California Press, 1990.

Hodgson, Godfrey. *The World Turned Right Side Up: A History of the Conservative Ascendancy in America.* Boston and New York: Houghton Mifflin, 1996.

———. *More Equal Than Others: America from Nixon to the New Century.* Princeton, N.J.: Princeton University Press, 2004.

Mickelthwait, John, and Adrian Wooldridge. *The Right Nation: Conservative Power in America.* New York: Penguin, 2004.

Nash, George H. *The Conservative Intellectual Movement in America since 1945.* New York: Basic Books, 1998.

Rusher, William A. *The Rise of the Right.* New York: William Morrow, 1984.

Schoenwald, Jonathan M. *A Time for Choosing: The Rise of Modern American Conservatism.* New York: Oxford University Press, 2001.

Siegel, Frederick F. *Troubled Journey: From Pearl Harbor to Ronald Reagan.* New York: Hill and Wang, 1984.

White, F. Clifton, and William J. Gill. *Why Reagan Won: A Narrative History of the Conservative Movement, 1964–1981.* Chicago: Regnery Gateway, 1981.

Williamson, Chilton, Jr. *The Conservative Bookshelf: Essential Works That Impact Today's Conservative Thinkers.* Secaucus, N.J.: The Citadel Press, 2004.

RELIGION

Allitt, Patrick. *Catholic Intellectuals and Conservative Politics in America, 1950–1985.* Ithaca, N.Y.: Cornell University Press, 1994.

Boyer, Peter. "The Big Tent: Billy Graham, Franklin Graham, and the Transformation of American Evangelicalism." *The New Yorker,* August 22, 2005.

Brown, Ruth Murray. *For a "Christian America": A History of the Religious Right.* Amherst, N.Y.: Prometheus Books, 2002.

Ezcurra, Ana Maria. *The Vatican and the Reagan Administration.* New York: CIRCUS Publications, 1986.

Fogel, Robert William. *The Fourth Great Awakening and the Future of Egalitarianism.* Chicago: University of Chicago Press, 2000.

Gorney, Cynthia. "Gambling with Abortion: Why Both Sides Think They Have Everything to Lose." *Harper's Magazine,* November 2004.

Heineman, Kenneth J. *God Is a Conservative: Religion, Politics, and Morality in Contemporary America.* New York and London: New York University Press, 1998.

Jorstad, Erling. *Evangelicals in the White House: The Cultural Maturation of Born Again Christianity, 1960–1981.* New York and Toronto: Edwin Mellen Press, 1981.

Kintz, Linda, and Julia Lesage, eds. *Media, Culture, and the Religious Right.* Minneapolis and London: University of Minnesota Press, 1998.

Lienesch, Michael. *Redeeming America: Piety and Politics in the New Christian Right.* Chapel Hill: University of North Carolina Press, 1993.

Martin, William. *With God on Our Side: The Rise of the Religious Right in America.* New York: Broadway, 1996.

Numbers, Ronald L. *The Creationists: From Scientific Creationism to Intelligent Design, Expanded Edition.* Cambridge, Mass.: Harvard University Press, 2006.

Reed, Ralph. *Active Faith: How Christians Are Changing the Soul of American Politics.* New York: The Free Press, 1996.

Utter, Glenn H., and John W. Storey, eds. *The Religious Right: A Reference Handbook*. Santa Barbara, Calif.: ABC-Clio, 1995.

Weaver, Mary Jo, and R. Scott Appleby, eds. *Being Right: Conservative Catholics in America*. Bloomington and Indianapolis: Indiana University Press, 1995.

Wills, Gary. "Fringe Government." *The New York Review of Books*, October 6, 2005.

BIOGRAPHIES AND MEMOIRS

Ambrose, Stephen. *Nixon*. Three volumes. New York: Simon and Schuster, 1989–1991.

Bass, Jack, and Marilyn W. Thompson. *Ol' Strom: An Unauthorized Biography of Strom Thurmond*. Atlanta: Longstreet, 1998.

Brady, John Joseph *Bad Boy: The Life and Politics of Lee Atwater*. New York: Perseus Books, 1997.

Carter, Dan T. *The Politics of Rage: George Wallace, the Origins of the New Conservatism, and the Transformation of American Politics*. Baton Rouge: Louisiana State University Press, 1995.

Critchlow, Donald. *Phyllis Schlafly and Grassroots Conservatism: A Woman's Crusade*. Princeton, N.J.: Princeton University Press, 2005.

Dobson, James, et al. *Seven Promises of a Promise Keeper*. Nashville, Tenn.: W Publishing Group, 1994.

Edwards, Lee. *Missionary for Freedom: The Life and Times of Walter Judd*. St. Paul, Minn.: Paragon House, 1990.

Felsonthal, Carol. *Phyllis Schlafly*. Washington, D.C.: Regnery Publishing, 1981.

Ferguson, Ernest B. *Hard Right: The Rise of Jesse Helms*. New York and London: W. W. Norton, 1986.

Frum, David. *The Right Man: The Surprise Presidency of George W. Bush*. New York: Random House, 2003.

Goldwater, Barry. *With No Apologies*. New York: William Morrow & Company, 1979.

Harrow, David E. *Pat Robertson: A Personal, Religious, and Political Portrait*. New York: Harper and Row, 1987.

Hicks, L. Edward. *"Sometimes in the Wrong, But Never in Doubt": George S. Benson and the Education of the New Religious Right*. Knoxville: University of Tennessee Press, 1994.

Jarvis, Howard. *I'm Mad as Hell: The Exclusive Story of the Tax Revolt and Its Leader*. New York: Times Books, 1979.

Judis, John H. *William F. Buckley, Jr.: Patron Saint of the Conservatives*. New York: Simon and Schuster, 1988.

LaHaye, Beverly. *The Restless Woman*. Grand Rapids, Mich.: Zondervan Publishing House, 1984.

Liebman, Marvin. *Coming Out Conservative.* San Francisco: Chronicle Books, 1992.

Perlstein, Rick. *Before the Storm: Barry Goldwater and the Unmaking of the American Consensus.* New York: Hill and Wang, 2001.

Phillips, Kevin. *American Dynasty: Aristocracy, Fortune and the Politics of Deceit in the House of Bush.* New York: Viking Adult, 2003.

Regnery, Henry. *Memoirs of a Dissident Publisher.* Washington, D.C.: Regnery Publishing, 1979.

Robertson, Pat. *The New World Order.* Dallas: Word Publishing, 1991.

Tygiel, Jules. *Ronald Reagan and the Triumph of American Conservatism.* Boston and New York: Longman Publishers, 2004.

Weber, Francis J. *His Eminence of Los Angeles: James Francis Cardinal McIntyre.* Los Angeles: Saint Francis Historical Society, 1997.

THE SOUTH

Aistrup, Joseph A. *The Southern Strategy Revisited: Republican Top-Down Advancement in the South.* Lexington: University of Kentucky Press, 1996.

Ammerman, Nancy Tatom. *Baptist Battles: Social Change and Religious Conflict in the Southern Baptist Convention.* Piscataway, N.J.: Rutgers University Press, 1990.

Bartley, Numan. *From Thurmond to Wallace: Political Tendencies in Georgia, 1948–1968.* Baltimore, Md.: The Johns Hopkins University Press, 1970.

Belknap, Michael R. *Federal Law and Southern Order: Racial Violence and Constitutional Conflict in the Post-Brown South.* Athens: University of Georgia Press, 1995.

Black, Earl, and Merle Black. *The Rise of Southern Republicanism.* Cambridge, Mass.: Harvard University Press, 2002.

Brattain, Michelle. *The Politics of Whiteness: Race, Workers, and Culture in the Modern South.* Athens and London: University of Georgia Press, 2004.

Clark, John A., and Charles Prysby, eds. *Southern Political Party Activists: Patterns of Conflict and Change, 1991–2001.* Lexington: University of Kentucky Press, 2004.

Feldman, Glenn, ed. *Before Brown: Civil Rights and White Backlash in the Modern South.* Tuscaloosa: University of Alabama Press, 2004.

Kruse, Kevin M. *White Flight: Atlanta and the Making of Modern Conservatism.* Princeton, N.J.: Princeton University Press, 2005.

Lassiter, Matthew. *Silent Majority: Suburban Politics in the Sunbelt South.* Princeton, N.J.: Princeton University Press, 2006.

Lind, Michael. *Made in Texas: George W. Bush and the Southern Takeover of American Politics.* New York: Basic Books, 2003.

McMillen, Neil. *Citizens' Council: Organized Resistance to the Second Reconstruction, 1954–1964*. Champaign: University of Illinois Press, 1971.

Schulman, Bruce J. *From Cotton Belt to Sunbelt: Federal Policy, Economic Development, and the Transformation of the South, 1938–1980*. New York: Oxford University Press, 1994.

Steed, Robert, Laurence Moreland, and Tod Baker, eds. *The 1984 Presidential Election in the South*. Westport, Conn.: Praeger Publishers, 1986.

Willis, Alan Scot. *All According to God's Plan: Southern Baptist Missions and Race, 1945–1970*. Lexington: University of Kentucky Press, 2005.

SPECIAL STUDIES

Andrew, John A., III. *The Other Side of the Sixties: Young Americans for Freedom and the Rise of Conservative Politics*. New Brunswick and London: Rutgers University Press, 1997.

Blumenthal, Sidney. *The Rise of the Counter-Establishment: From Conservative Ideology to Political Power*. New York: Harper and Row Perennial Library, 1988.

Brock, David. *The Republican Noise Machine*. New York: Three Rivers, 2004.

Burkett, Elinor. *The Right Women: A Journey through the Heart of Conservative America*. New York: Touchstone, 1998.

Daalder, Ivo H., and James Lindsay. *America Unbound: The Bush Revolution in Foreign Policy*. New York: John Wiley and Sons, 2003.

Dorrien, Gary. *The Neo-Conservative Mind: Politics, Culture, and the War of Ideology*. Philadelphia: Temple University Press, 1993.

Edwards, Lee. *The Power of Ideas: The Heritage Foundation at 25 Years*. Ottawa, Ill.: Jameson Books, 1997.

Frank, Thomas. *What's the Matter with Kansas?: How the Conservatives Won the Heart of America*. New York: Basic Books, 2004.

Goldfield, Michael. *The Decline of Organized Labor in the United States*. Chicago: University of Chicago Press, 1987.

Hart, Jeffrey. *The Making of the American Conservative Mind:* National Review *and Its Times*. Wilmington, Del.: Intercollegiate Studies Institute, 2005.

Hoeveler, J. David. *Watch on the Right: Conservative Intellectuals in the Reagan Era*. Madison: University of Wisconsin Press, 1991.

McGirr, Lisa. *Suburban Warriors: The Origins of the New American Right*. Princeton, N.J.: Princeton University Press, 2001.

Mendelberg, Tali. *The Race Card: Campaign Strategy, Implicit Messages, and the Norm of Equality*. Princeton, N.J.: Princeton University Press, 2001.

Sabato, Larry. *Feeding Frenzy: Attack Journalism and American Politics*. Baltimore, Md.: Lanahan, 1991.

Scatamburlo, Valerie L. *Soldiers of Misfortune: The New Right's Culture War and the Politics of Political Correctness.* New York: Grove/Atlantic, 1998.

Schneider, Gregory L. *Cadres for Conservatism: Young Americans for Freedom and the Rise of the Contemporary Right.* New York and London: New York University Press, 1999.

Sugrue, Thomas. *Origins of the Urban Crisis.* Princeton, N.J.: Princeton University Press, 1996.

Viguerie, Richard A., and David Francke, eds. *America's Right Turn: How Conservatives Used New and Alternative Media to Take Power.* Chicago and New York: Bonus Books, 2004.

WEBSITES

Nearly every figure featured in the documents sections and many of the organizations and periodicals mentioned in the introduction and headnotes have their own Web sites or a Wikipedia entry with relevant links.

Acknowledgments (continued from p. iv)

Document 1. David Lawrence, "America Turns the Corner," The United States News, July 11, 1947. Copyrighted 2013. U.S. News & World Report. 106329:1213JM. Reprinted by permission.

Document 5. From the book *The Conservative Mind: From Burke to Santayana* by Russell Kirk. Copyright © 1985. Published by Regnery Publishing, Inc. All rights reserved. Reprinted by special permission of Regnery Publishing Inc., Washington, D.C.

Document 6. William F. Buckley Jr., "Publisher's Statement on Founding National Review." © 1955 by National Review, Inc. Reprinted by permission.

Document 7. "Why the South Must Prevail." © 1957 by National Review, Inc. Reprinted by permission.

Document 9. From the book *The Conscience of a Conservative* by Barry Goldwater. Copyright © 1990. Published by Regnery Publishing, Inc.

Document 10. Young Americans for Freedom, "The Sharon Statement." © 1960 by National Review, Inc. Reprinted by permission.

Document 11. Milton Friedman, excerpt from *Capitalism and Freedom.* © University of Chicago Press, 2002. Reprinted by permission. © 1962, 1982, 2002 by The University of Chicago. All rights reserved.

Document 12. Ronald Reagan, "Rendezvous with Destiny." Reprinted by permission of Ronald Reagan Presidential Foundation & Library.

Document 13. L. Brent Bozell, "Who is Accommodating to What?" © 1965 by National Review, Inc. Reprinted by permission.

Document 14. "George Wallace for President" brochure. Courtesy of 4president.org.

Document 16. Frank S. Meyer, "Defense of the Republic." © 1970 by National Review, Inc. Reprinted by permission.

Document 17. Donald Atwell Zoll, "Capital Punishment." © 1971 by National Review, Inc. Reprinted by permission.

Document 18. Lewis F. Powell Jr., "Confidential Memorandum: Attack on American Free Enterprise System." Courtesy of ReclaimDemocracy.org.

Document 19. "You in a Heap o'Trouble, Son." © Jeff MacNelly Editorial, © 1972 MacNelly—Distributed by King Features Syndicate, Inc.

Document 21. "Act Before It Is Too Late." Reprinted with permission of *The American Rifleman* magazine, September 1974 issue. Copyright National Rifle Association of America, 2013.

Document 22. From *Affirmative Discrimination* by Nathan Glazer, copyright © 1975. Reprinted by permission of Basic Books, a member of the Perseus Books Group.

Document 23. Alan Crawford, "The Taxfighters Are Coming!" Courtesy of Alan Crawford. Reprinted with permission.

Document 24. Phyllis Schlafly, "Interview." From *The Washington Post*, January 18, 1976, © 1976 Washington Post Company. All rights Reserved. Used by permission and protected by the Copyright Laws of the United States. The printing, copying, redistribution, or retransmission of this Content without express written permission is prohibited.

Document 25. Committee on the Present Danger, "Common Sense and the Common Danger." Washington D.C.: Pergamon-Brassey's Publishers, 1984.

Index